The Fatal Equilibrium

The Fatal Equilibrium

Marshall Jevons

The MIT Press
Cambridge, Massachusetts
London, England

Excerpts from "The Song of Commodity," by Bertolt
Brecht, are reprinted by permission from "The Measures
Taken," in *The Measures Taken and Other Lehrstücke*,
translated by Carl R. Mueller (London: Methuen & Co.,
Ltd., 1977); English translation copyright 1977 by
Methuen & Co., Ltd.; in German, rights owned by
Suhrkamp Verlag.

T. S. Eliot, "The Hollow Men." From "The Hollow
Men" in *Collected Poems 1909–1962* by T. S. Eliot, copyright 1936 by Harcourt Brace Jovanovich, Inc.; copyright
1963, 1964 by T. S. Eliot. For the U.S.A., reprinted by
permission of Faber and Faber Ltd.

"Soon," by George and Ira Gershwin, © 1929 (re-
newed) New World Music Corporation. All rights reserved. Used by permission.

This book was set in Palatino by The MIT Press Com-
putergraphics Department and printed and bound by
Halliday Lithograph in the United States of America.

Library of Congress Cataloging in Publication Data

Jevons, Marshall.
  The fatal equilibrium.
  I. Title.
PS3560.E88F3   1985   813'.54   85-4313
ISBN 0-262-10032-0

Contents

The Fatal Equilibrium

What is rice anyway?
Do I know what rice is?
How should I know who should know?
I don't know what rice is.
All I know is its price.

What is cotton anyway?
Do I know what cotton is?
How should I know who should know?
I don't know what cotton is.
All I know is its price.

What is Man anyway?
Do I know what Man is?
How should I know who should know?
I don't know what Man is.
All I know is his price.

—Bertolt Brecht, excerpts from "The Song of Commodity"

Flashforward
Thursday, January 10

A small syringe lay at the center of the rosewood desk. Only the soft light of a desk lamp illuminated the area around it. Several fountain pens and letter openers, a magnifying glass, and assorted clips, fasteners, erasers, and tweezers surrounded the space that had been cleared for the translucent instrument. The object appeared incongruous on the reddish, black-streaked surface of the polished wood. Indeed the syringe was out of harmony with the room itself.

A maroon chenille carpet covered the floor beneath the desk, and drapes of a deeper hue bracketed the two tall windows that faced the street below. The mulberry silk cushions on the window box matched the fabric on a corner settee. Logs burned in the open fireplace casting gray shadows on the cream wallpaper, all but hiding its design of light gilt fleurs-de-lis. On the marble mantel a glass menagerie of circus animals looked impassively at the motionless person seated before the desk. Several minutes passed. The syringe was now encased in the fingers of its owner. Slowly, methodically, the plunger was drawn to suck five cc's of colorless liquid into the small cylinder. Labored breathing was the only sound in the room.

The empty vial was then concealed in the rear of a drawer, lost in the unsorted paraphernalia of the drawer's contents. The syringe itself was lifted to eye level and examined against the light of the lamp. The calibration showed enough fluid to achieve the intended result.

"Foolish, that's the word for it. And stubborn. It didn't have to be this way at all." But the decision was made. And tonight would set in train steps that were necessary to bring an end to the affair. It was almost 11:00. The date was January 10th, exactly a month since the intrusions into a previously secure world had begun. A cashmere scarf and heavy coat were donned to prepare for the cold walk. It had all been rehearsed earlier.

The ebbing fire was left untended as the figure made its way down the staircase to the front room. A standing lamp by the front door provided the light for a final and critical action. A pair of loose-fitting cotton gloves were produced from the coat pocket; they were too thin for the cold and snowy New England night.

The left glove was put on. Then the syringe was inserted cautiously and maneuvered between the fabric of the glove and the index finger. The point was carefully positioned to protrude only slightly through the seam at the tip of the glove's finger. The cotton fabric provided no resistance to the needle. A motion that had been practiced several times could now complete the task. Bending the palm of the hand toward the fingers would force the sliding plunger to do its job.

Most of the junior faculty at Harvard wanted to live in Cambridge. The heady intellectual atmosphere of North America's most prominent educational center made dwelling in one of Boston's numerous bedroom communities an un-attractive alternative. Cambridge not only offered the libraries of Harvard and MIT, and a host of other intellectual resources, but its shops and restaurants and bookstores were exceeded

in their diversity only by the manifold array of cultural opportunities. Lectures, the performing arts, and exhibits rotated
constantly through the academic calendar.

Living in this city was not inexpensive. For the most part
only senior faculty occupied the large single houses on the
northwest side of the university. For impecunious and transient
assistant professors, apartments and townhouses to the east
were the order of the day.

Dennis Gossen considered himself fortunate to live in one
such apartment. He had made it his home from the first day
he had arrived at Harvard five years earlier. And the depressing
thought that he would have to leave had now been driven
from his mind. This was a time to relish. He had never entertained doubts that he deserved to remain at Harvard. But
now he held in his hand the envelope that he knew would
assure his stay there. The Dean thoughtfully had seen to it
that each candidate learned the results of the promotion and
tenure committee's deliberations on the very day of their ap-
proval by the President's office, however late in the evening
that sometimes turned out to be. The important news was
distributed by messenger. Gossen's notice had just arrived,
but he did not rush to open it. Instead he took pleasure in
contemplating its contents. It had taken long years of hard
work to get this far. There would be time enough to savor
the moment. The envelope would for now remain unopened.

In spite of the way Gossen had come to fit with his job at
Harvard, in appearance he stood apart from most of his peers.
Boyish beyond his thirty years, he had a small thin frame
and a youthful demeanor that was augmented by a tan even
five years of Massachusetts' winters had not erased. Even his
clothes remained Californian and stood out in bright contrast
to the drab colors that characterized the attire of most young

Cambridge academicians. A chemistry major in college, Gossen did not take an economics course until his senior year. After that, chemistry became a hobby. Economics became a calling. Notwithstanding his meager undergraduate training in the subject, five years ago he had been the top graduate student in economics at Stanford. And he had been a hot property in the job market that year. The call to Harvard could not have been resisted.

This was not to say there had not been drawbacks to the decision to accept the position at Harvard. Other institutions vying for his services had offered him more salary. And he had been told that the prospect for an assistant professor to be promoted and kept on at Harvard was remote. When Harvard wanted to fill a senior faculty slot, it canvassed the entire country in search of the top scholar in the field. A junior member of the Harvard faculty was in competition, therefore, not only with his or her peers at Harvard but with established scholars elsewhere of world-class reputation. Gossen knew he was in this league. The other assistant professors, he thought, both here and elsewhere, did not surpass him in intellectual prowess. And his published output already had begun to establish him solidly in his field.

The niche Gossen had carved for himself was in the relatively new area of the economics of information. Originating at the University of Chicago, this field of economics had affected work at all major centers of learning. Information theory originally concerned the process by which consumers and workers sought and gained the information necessary to make their transactions. And transactions, after all, are ultimately the subject matter of economics: buyers and sellers seeking and finding each other in order to exchange goods and services.

Gossen and his fellow transaction-cost analysts reveled in exploring and modeling all this seeking and finding. To the surprise of many economists, the economics of information turned out to have eye-opening implications for the traditional approach to product quality, the futures market, unemployment policy, the role of advertising, and other economic problems as well.

Most economists had spun their models as if the cost of information were zero. But information now was recognized as a useful commodity, like a drill press or a can of corn, that gave its holder something of value: knowledge. And like any good, economists reasoned, it will be collected so long as the value of the information is greater than the cost of acquiring it.

Gossen focused on information in labor markets where the information sought is the possible existence of a higher wage offer. It may seem obvious that the cost of finding out is the time, effort, and bother of seeking a higher paying job, but Gossen discovered a not-so-obvious consequence in this.

As Gossen told his students, when they go out to find their first jobs, those seeking occupations where employers offer a wide variety of wages for the same work will find it to their advantage to search longer and harder for a job. Why? Because the worker knows that the next job interview may entail a salary higher than that offered at the last interview. Where employers are all offering similar salaries, the chance that a person will be offered a higher paying job at the next interview is less than it would be if there were a great variety of wages offered. And since the cost of searching would be the same in both occupations, workers will look longer for jobs where wages are not closely bunched. So where would there be the most unemployment? Gossen concluded this would occur in those occupations where salaries were all over the board. And his statistics showed he was right.

Gossen's skills at collecting numbers and interpreting them through the lens of economic theory were admired by his colleagues; and his counsel was sought regularly by graduate students in need of these talents to complete doctoral dissertations. His research efforts had been very fruitful.

There had been some rough spots in his teaching as Gossen acclimated himself to occupying the front of a classroom after some twenty years of being seated near the back. But his graduate seminar on the economics of information was now well attended, and even his undergraduate teaching of economic principles was well received.

There was another reason to be glad over the decision to come to Cambridge. Her name was Melissa. Melissa Shannon. The thought of the name could soften his countenance. He had been introduced to her one evening when he had taken another member of the faculty to a play. Once he had met her, all thought of other relationships stopped.

Melissa was not associated with the university, something Gossen appreciated about her. His work was put aside when they were together. There was no need to be on guard, intellectually alert against any verbal expression that revealed a flaw in his brain's logical reasoning or a gap in its factual inventory. Melissa was a temporary and welcome relief from all this. He had asked her six months ago to marry him. After many ups and downs, and wavering on her part, she had recently said yes.

The young economist rose from the chair of his Fayette Street apartment and crossed the hardwood floor into the small kitchen. He opened a cabinet beside the sink where he

kept a bit of scotch, sherry, and vodka. His expected visitor
might want to share a toast with him. He was looking forward
with excitement to his late-night rendezvous. Things had not
always gone well between them. But that, he pursuaded himself, was in the past.

He walked into the living room with two glasses and put
them on the small coffee table before a dowdy fabric couch.
He looked around disapprovingly at the other furniture that
came with the apartment. The one item in which Gossen took
some pride of possession was a Barcelona chair, whose graceful
lines contrasted sharply with its surroundings. The chair had
been a college graduation present from his parents. They were
both architects in Santa Barbara and believed deeply that the
presence of a Barcelona chair guaranteed one's cachet as avant-
garde.

Gossen strolled over to the far end of the living room,
where the chair was positioned kitty-corner from the entrance
to the apartment. Taking a book at random from the adjacent
wall rack, he settled himself into the black leather and chrome
extravagance. He flipped through the pages without interest.
His eyes wandered and suddenly fixed upon the poster that
hung on his east wall. It had been designed for the Rodin
exhibit at the National Gallery and depicted a detail from The
Gates of Hell. Gossen was reminded of the inscription on the
entrance to Dante's *Inferno*, "All hope abandon ye who enter
here." A motto, he mused, for most assistant professors
brought on to the Harvard faculty.

Other junior faculty made light of abandoning all hope for
promotion at this institution. And in Gossen's mind, he knew
it was no disgrace not to be retained. Indeed many academic
institutions recruited avidly the about-to-be released members
of Harvard's faculty. But in his heart Gossen would have been

mortified by his first failure. He wanted to retain the imprimatur of being a Harvard professor. If he ever left Cambridge, he wanted it to be on his own terms.

The cotton glove grasping the bannister moved slowly upward. The only sound in the hall was the breathing, slightly harder than normal after the exertions of the walk through the snow that by now covered the streets and sidewalks of Cambridge. In the last few minutes the snow had begun to come down faster, making walking increasingly difficult.

Upward, upward, and slowly upward, then a hesitation. There was still time to turn back. Nothing irremediable had been done. From deep within the recesses of memory, a half-forgotten poem came to mind.

> Between the idea
> And the reality
> Between the motion
> And the act
> Falls the Shadow

The light from the fixture above the stairs was dim, and the grayness of the corridor helped conceal the peculiar position of the left glove. This hand was favored, held close to the body for protection. The grip of the right hand on the stair railing was firm.

> Between the conception
> And the creation
> Between the emotion
> And the response
> Falls the Shadow

The person on the stairs stopped suddenly. A door to an apartment on the first landing was held ajar. From the stairs, an eye could be seen glancing out the doorway, the door's chain still in place. "Anyone there?" From the shadows there came no response.

The door was hastily closed again. The clicking sound of a deadbolt being secured was audible in the stairway.

> The eyes are not here
> There are no eyes here
> In this valley of dying stars

The presence on the stairs remained motionless. Then the upward progress resumed. Step by step the second landing came closer. The ascent became quieter as the sound of breathing returned to normal. Fortuitously the stairs did not creak. And the carpet, though threadbare, muffled any squeaking from the visitor's boots, now dripping from their collection of melting snow.

> Between the desire
> And the spasm
> Between the potency
> And the existence
> Between the essence
> And the descent
> Falls the Shadow

The shadow of a gloved hand fell across the nameplate on the apartment door. An index finger moved beneath the name to verify the identity of the dweller within. Remorseless eyes gazed upon the cold script. The hunt was ended.

The hand that held the needle was given a final scrutiny. A tiny glint showed from the tip of the glove's index finger. The hand was returned to its place close to the midsection of the winter coat.

Dennis Gossen's impatient pacing, as he awaited his tardy

guest, was halted by the gusty ring of the doorbell. He turned in the direction of the doorway. A slight smile crossed his lips. At the last moment, before he swung open the door, he felt a sudden twinge of anxiety. Gossen pulled the door toward him with anticipation. He smiled a greeting, waved his visitor in, and closed the door once again.

"I have some sherry for us." And Gossen proceeded to lead his guest toward the refreshments. The young economist saw ahead of him the sparkle of the decanter and glasses. Then he felt the sting of the needle in his shoulder. The sherry decanter suddenly rose into the air and hung suspended. Then he saw nothing. His body lay motionless upon the floor.

> This is the way the world ends
> Not with a bang but a whimper.

1
Friday, December 21

"Orderly mind, disorderly desk," Henry Spearman thought to himself as his hands burrowed through the papers in front of him. "Where is that memo?" he muttered. He was soon to find it under a manila folder containing last semester's lecture notes. He sat back in his chair and studied the message he had just retrieved.

> TO: Members of the P & T Committee
> FROM: Denton Clegg, Dean
> This is the schedule for our committee's deliberations:
> Tuesday, January 8: 1:00 p.m.–7:00 p.m.
> Wednesday, January 9: 9:00 a.m.–2:00 p.m.
> I trust everyone will have read the relevant material pertaining to the candidates by that time. Let me remind you again of the confidentiality of this material and of our deliberations.

Spearman reached into his breast pocket for his date book and jotted the information down. Christmas break would be no vacation for members of the promotion and tenure committee. At least not if they did their homework. Spearman winced when he thought of the manuscripts he had yet to read and the letters of recommendation about candidates he had yet to decipher. A straightforward letter was a thing of the past, the victim of a litigious age. The real letter was written between the lines—what was left unsaid was often more important than what was said. But what was said provided hints as to what was left out. To be told that a candidate had a good personality was a substitute for not being told of the candidate's shortcomings in scholarly potential. To say that someone was effective in the classroom was a euphemism for their being defective in research. Spearman was not looking forward to reading those letters any more than most of the manuscripts that awaited him.

It was the responsibility of the promotion and tenure committee at Harvard to evaluate candidates from all fields in the arts and sciences. Spearman felt uneasy making such consequential judgments about faculty members outside of his own specialty. His specialty was economics, a subject that did not enlighten him on the merits of an art historian or biochemist. Yet that is what he had to do, and of course every other member of the committee was in the same boat.

The ring of the phone interrupted his thoughts. It was Pidge.

"No," he told her, "I'm going to grab a bite in the Square this evening. I've got work on the promotion committee I want to do." Henry Spearman hung up his phone. He wanted to get the remaining manuscripts of the promotion candidates before the Dean's office closed. So he started in the direction of Clegg's office. It was going to be a long night.

Pidge Spearman replaced the receiver. "I wonder if Adam Smith knew what he started," she mused. The founder of the discipline of economics had written about specialization of labor in pin factories, the invisible hand, and the benefits from free trade. Seemingly Adam Smith had begun only an academic discipline, a social science. But to Pidge Spearman, spouse of an economics professor, Smith had begun much more than a branch of learning. He also had created a career that was now for many of its practitioners a fully absorbing one. It was a career with its own rules of behavior, its own pecking order, and its own conventions. Her husband was one who followed these rules and conventions and currently was at the top of the pecking order.

Pidge Spearman's childhood in an academic household had not fully prepared her for life with an economist. Professors she grew up with as a child, and professors in other departments at Harvard whom she and her husband enjoyed socially, were serious about their work. But they did not insert their academic specialties into every nook and cranny of life.

Pidge walked into the living room and drew the curtains. December nights came early in Cambridge. The streetlight near their house had already gone on. "This might be a good time to see Jessica about that little matter," she thought. But the decision was deferred by the ring of the doorbell.

"That's the back door," she said to herself. "Usually only Henry comes in that way." She went toward the kitchen, but with some reluctance. Their home in Cambridge fronted on expensive real estate. The houses were stately Victorian dwellings, built at the turn of the century. But an alleyway ran behind these homes that was in marked contrast to the neatly tended lawns. Run-down garages, debris, yard trimmings, and garbage cans lined the common driveway.

Pidge's halting steps brought her to the back door. The casement curtain that covered the door window allowed her to see only a silhouette. She could not make out who it was. With cautious fingertips, she parted the curtain and peeked out. A young man stood on the doorstep. His breath, like jets of smoke, merged into the icy air. He was underdressed for the winter weather: a light jacket and no gloves or boots, though a trooper cap protected the top of his head.

Pidge recognized him as a junior colleague of her husband's, someone she had seen in the department office but had never met. Should she open the door to a stranger? His obvious discomfort decided the question for her.

"Forgive me, Mrs. Spearman. My name is Dennis Gossen." He seemed embarrassed and avoided eye contact with her. "I know we've not met, but I teach in the Economics department with your husband. I very much hope he's at home and that I can see him." He affected a quick smile.

"I'm sorry, he isn't here. But come in and warm yourself a moment. I'm afraid Henry won't be home until late. He said he was going to do some committee work at the office. You could find him there, but I'm not sure he'd want to be interrupted. Of course, if it's terribly important. . ."

"Oh, it is, Mrs. Spearman. And it's confidential too. That's why I came to your back door. I suspect your husband's work tonight involves the committee on promotion and tenure. I'm up for tenure this year, and so I'm not supposed to have personal contact with people like your husband. But there's something he needs to know."

"Let me make you some tea. It will warm you up." Pidge insisted her visitor stay before sending him off to find her husband.

The young man sipped his tea silently. He believed no one had seen him make this visit, an accomplishment that would be more difficult if he were to approach Spearman in his office. Harvard's Littauer Center housed professors and graduate students who could be found working on or debating economic research at any time of the day or night. He asked Mrs. Spearman if he could wait until her husband returned.

"It may be several hours," she replied. "But let me call and tell him you are here. Maybe he could come home earlier."

Gossen hesitated while he thought about this proposition.

Normally he would not have wanted to be the cause of a disruption in the routine of a tenured professor. But in this instance he felt he had no choice. He asked Pidge Spearman to call her husband.

Spearman was at that time entering Mowbray Hall, where he climbed the stairs to the second-floor office of Dean Clegg. There he gathered a tall stack of papers, over twenty pounds in weight, he estimated, which were to be his homework for that night and the next several days. These were the remaining articles, monographs, reviews, and books authored by the candidates for promotion. It was on the basis of the words and numbers and formulae on these pages, and primarily on these alone, that aspiring professors' tenure at Harvard would be determined. The short, balding professor struggled down the stairs with his load.

"Let me give you a hand with that, Henry. That looks heavy."

"It's not heavy; it's my bother," Spearman quipped. "And besides, you'll be bothered with a similar load once you leave the Dean's office."

Spearman's would-be Good Samaritan was Professor Morrison Bell of the Mathematics department. He too was a member of the promotion and tenure committee. His purpose in visiting Mowbray Hall was the same as Spearman's.

Morrison Bell was the star of the Mathematics department. In terms of pecking order, his position was comparable to that of Spearman's in Economics. But in almost every other respect, there was little resemblance. Morrison Bell was easily a foot taller than Spearman and a man of different mood and vintage. Whereas Spearman spent no time on his wardrobe, Bell cultivated the menswear shops of Cambridge. His straight dark hair was slicked back and curled up at the collar. He was sloe-eyed and his thin face was dark complexioned. He spoke in measured tones but had the disconcerting trait of forming his words with his lips a small but perceptible moment before the sound consonant with that lip movement emerged. This gave his listeners the impression of watching a film whose sound track was slightly out of sync. In his lectures Bell's students at first believed that something was amiss, that somehow their ears were not synchronized properly with their eyes.

Professor Bell was relieved to know that his offer of help had been declined. He was anxious to pick up the copies of the same material and settle in for a long siege of study. Having Spearman on the promotion committee this year, he knew, was not going to make the deliberations progress any easier. The economist was thought to be argumentative and nit-picking by scholars in more traditional disciplines. But one man's mote was another man's beam.

Still, Bell admired the logic-chopping professor, knowing that standards for research would not be lessened under Spearman's scrutiny. Indeed, Spearman would be a welcome counterpoint to Foster Barrett from the Classics department. Barrett's criterion for promotion was not pure scholarship. The candidate's social position was also given great weight. An only average assistant professor might be deemed superior by Foster Barrett if he or she were a Lodge, a Cabot, or a Lowell. Bell knew of Spearman's lineage: a child of impecunious Jewish immigrants. Spearman would place no stock in such stock.

Bell loped up the stairs in the direction of the Dean's office. Spearman struggled down the same stairs as he began the trek to his office where a phone's persistent ring drew no response.

2
Friday, December 21

The fading evening sunlight cast large shadows from the trees outside the house and darkened the room in which Valerie Danzig was reading. The gray of dusk contrasted starkly with the bright chrome and clear fixtures that furnished the room. The east and west walls of the living room were flat white, but the spines of hundreds of books shelved neatly from floor to ceiling on the adjacent walls lent flashes of color, compatible with the Mark Rothko hanging opposite her chair. Visitors who ventured from this room into any other might wonder if they had entered another house. Each room had been decorated individually. Bauhaus modern, country antique, Victorian, Mediterranean, and colonial: the Danzig dwelling embraced them all, protecting the occupant from any ennui a single style might engender.

"This won't do, this won't do at all," she murmured as she reached for the switch on the floor lamp. Professor Danzig set aside the article she had been reading, that of a young sociologist at Harvard. She had not liked what she considered the superficial use of Freud to develop a psychosociological explanation of bureaucratic decision-making.

"Is anyone on the committee from 'Sosh'?" she wondered. To satisfy herself, she reopened the manila folder containing Dean Clegg's memo informing her of the formation of the promotion and tenure committee and of her inclusion. A glance at the list of designates reminded her that Oliver Wu had been chosen by Clegg from that department.

"Probably Wu will support his own department's candidate," she thought. Danzig knew that a candidate who had been recommended to the P and T committee had already been scrutinized by that person's own department. Every article, every book, every review, indeed usually every unpublished paper will have had a peer review at the department level and even this assessment was not enough. There were also the evaluations of outside authorities.

It was only in the case of departments badly divided over personalities, ideologies, or methodologies that a candidate for promotion who had gotten as far as consideration by the P and T committee might not be unanimously supported by the senior faculty in that field. But normally one dissenting vote from a respected full professor was enough to scotch a candidate's name from being put forward. Danzig did not know Wu personally. But she knew enough of his reputation to conjecture that if he disliked a junior scholar's work, that person had little chance for being kept on.

But the strategy by which Wu could accomplish this goal might be Byzantine. A member of the P and T committee had an enormous advantage over departmental colleagues in determining a junior colleague's fate. Wu might not have showed his hand during departmental deliberations in order to maintain good relations with the candidate's supporters, and even with the candidiate. Later he could with impunity play the role of the heavy on the Dean's committee, where his voice would carry great weight but with more assurance that the proceedings and his impact upon them would be held in confidence.

But regardless of her Sociology colleague's disposition toward the matter, Danzig knew her vote was negative. This was an outrageous attempt to claim the authority of Freud for what was in fact a gross misapplication of his work. She quickly wrote her critique, which she hoped would send this young scholar away from Cambridge.

Weary from an entire day spent reading, Professor Danzig decided to review the file of one more candidate, and then break off for a late dinner. "Might as well make it the thinnest one," she said under her breath as she turned to the floor where she had placed each candidate's output and letters of recommendation. There were an even dozen such stacks remaining for her consideration. The shortest stack was readily identified.

"Is there enough here on which to make a decision," she wondered as she placed the file on her lap. The psychologist knew that a mere counting of the pages was not the basis for judgment. Unfortunately, she sighed, one had to read what was there before rendering a decision. Still, the paucity of material surprised her, since the candidate was in the field of economics, one of Harvard's strongest departments. Any candidate endorsed by them should be competitive with the candidates fielded by less confident departments.

"Dennis Gossen." To her surprise, she actually knew someone outside her department who was a candidate for promotion. How inconvenient it should be Dennis Gossen. A half-smile crossed her lips. She leaned back in her chair, remembering their earlier evenings together. Perhaps she should disqualify herself from the deliberations in this instance. But then why should she? No one on the promotion and tenure committee would know of their connection. It was, after all, so unlikely. To be included among the senior faculty at an institution like Harvard required an extraordinary dedication to one's discipline. This precluded much socializing with those outside one's specialty. After fifteen years on the staff, Professor Danzig could count on two hands the number of faculty outside of Psychology with whom she had significant social contact.

It was even less likely that she would know an untenured professor in another department. There was a social hierarchy that defined one's caste in the Ivy League. The untenured were the untouchables of a university's caste system. And while not as severe as untouchability in India, a breakdown of this social organization would require a figure of no less than Gandhian proportions.

The Gossen file contained the reprints of six slender articles, accompanied by a letter from the chairman of the Economics department summarizing the views of Gossen's senior colleagues on his work. Completing the file was the correspondence the department had had with three economists not at Harvard who were requested to assess the candidate's qualifications.

As had been her practice thus far, Valerie Danzig read first the outside letters. The letters were uniformly strong. But they were read reservedly by Danzig. Based upon the experience in her own department, she knew that one should not rely only on external appraisals. It was no secret that outside letters were not always drawn randomly from top scholars in a candidate's field but could be carefully selected in hopes of eliciting a response consistent with the desires of the faction controlling the department.

She then skimmed the lengthy letter from Leonard Kost, the chairman of Gossen's department. It was a straightforward summary of each tenured professor's view on the candidate, with particular devotion to the handful who specialized in

Gossen's fields of expertise. The views were positive, without exception.

The first reprint Danzig prepared herself to read was bound in a deep red cover, recognizable to the cognoscenti as being from a leading American journal in economics. She read the conclusions first, then examined the equations that preceded them.

"Does Dennis really believe people behave this way?" Valerie Danzig murmured to herself. She had by now made her way through half of the short stack of papers. Their pattern was becoming clear. In each instance Gossen had accepted a view of human beings that was contradictory to what modern psychology knew about human nature. To the psychologist, mankind was complex and motivated by many contradictory impulses. The irrational was as likely to determine a man or woman's actions as was cold-blooded logic.

Gossen on the other hand premised all of his work on the assumption that people had only one goal in mind in all of their doings. It appeared to her to be the single-minded pursuit of happiness. This is what she could not abide in the young scholar's work.

Valerie Danzig's own research specialty was the psychological behavior of the gifted child. A disciple of the Russian psychologist Vygotsky, she had written a book, *The Muse and the Fire of Genius*, that was now the standard authority in the field. For most of her professional career, she had met virtually every Monday, Wednesday, and Friday with a selection of the most quick-witted children in the Boston–Cambridge area. Her stated agenda to their parents was to expose these sons and daughters to the world of books and ideas at a level far beyond the resources of the local school. Her unstated agenda was to monitor the learning patterns and stimulus-response mechanisms of these prodigies as they were exposed to advanced studies in the calculus, statistical inference, and musical theory.

Danzig was persuaded that by studying young children one could discover the forms of adult thought. And by studying only the best and the brightest, she had long ago concluded one could understand the highest forms of adult behavior. An adult, after all, was but a child grown large.

The children she studied clinically were demure yet flamboyant, innocent but also cunning, brilliant while still naive, cheerful yet petulant. Unimpressed, yet utterly impressionable, they were as likely to be influenced by Mozart as by Madison Avenue. Acutely perceptive, they were nonetheless often confused. She could not imagine how one could attribute to the thought processes of these gifted children, nor to the adults they would become, the computer-like rationality of Gossen's model.

When Valerie Danzig was irritated, she took her relief by heading toward the refrigerator. That it did not take much to exasperate the eminent psychologist was intimated by her girth. Just a snack before dinner, she thought, as she made a beeline for the kitchen. Out came the bread, the mayonnaise, and the sliced turkey. Rapidly combining them, she snatched a Coke and was soon back at her desk where she resumed her reading of Gossen's work.

"Economic man," she harumphed. "Here he is again, Thorstein Veblen's lightning calculator of pleasures and pains reincarnated in the work of a supposedly modern social scientist." She wondered why Veblen's ridicule of economic man, coming after all from within the ranks of economists themselves, had not been sufficient to end the use of this caricature. She swallowed the last corner of her sandwich and downed her Coke.

Her own field of psychology had long ago branched off from its roots in utilitarianism. No modern psychologist today was persuaded that people sought only to maximize their own personal utility in all that they did. Utility, Danzig thought, was an archaic catchall for happiness or pleasure or satisfaction or some such emotion. The term had no content. Whatever you did, you presumably maximized your utility. Did you kiss your husband or did you cheat on him? Did you pet your dog or did you scold your dog? Did you purchase a new Rolls or a used Chevy? It didn't matter! You chose whatever made you happiest. How can we tell it made you happiest? Because that's what you chose. And why did you choose it? Because it made you happy. To a psychologist like Danzig, this was reasoning in a circle. It was a theory that was no more than a tautology. Economics merely says that people do what they do.

Valerie Danzig then prepared to do what she would do. A note was clipped to the Gossen file. It was brief, containing only three words: vote to reject. As she placed the stack of material back on the carpet with the folders of the other candidates, she found herself muttering, "There are more things in Heaven and earth, Mr. Dennis Gossen, than are dreamt of in your philosophy."

3
Friday, December 21

The phone was ringing when Spearman reached his office door. He dropped the bundle of books and papers on the hallway floor and fumbled through his overcoat pocket for the key to Littauer 413. The economist made it to his office phone slightly out of breath but in time to hear the voice of his wife. "Henry, I'm sorry to interrupt you again. I know you wanted to work all evening. But there's someone here who wants to see you."

"Is Patricia home already?" he asked.

"No, I don't really expect her until late tonight. It's Dennis Gossen—the young man from your department. He's in the living room now and he seems very anxious to talk to you. I told him you were working, but he said the matter was so important and he didn't want to see you at the office. Anyway, he's here and I told him I would try and call you."

"Did he say why?"

"Not to me. He just said it was urgent that he see you. He does seem distressed. And I don't doubt that he is. He came over on such a cold night."

"Well, I'm reluctant to come home. It means an end to my work here. And I'm not sure I ought to see him either. Do you think I should come home?"

"I'd appreciate it if you would. He's not going to leave until you do and I want to pick up some things at Sage's before Patty arrives."

Henry Spearman reluctantly agreed to come home. The short, balding professor took off his horn-rimmed spectacles and defogged them with his handkerchief. He did not handle interruptions gracefully. But that was his own choice. To Spearman the economist, one chose one's disposition the way one chooses any commodity—through a comparison of costs and benefits. At one time in his life interruptions of this sort were met with greater cheer. But at that time in his career, he gave up less income when he allowed himself to be diverted into other pursuits. Therefore, interruptions entailed fewer costs.

Now he was one of the stars of Harvard's Economics department. And paradoxically, with the rise in his income, he felt less able to afford interruptions and diversions. He earned large sums from his public lectures, guest columns in the print media, and the sales of his books. To go home now would mean the loss of four hours of work on his P and T assignment. To make this up would mean the loss of four hours' work on a lecture or column or book. So the cost of the interuption might be a column in a news magazine for which he would receive a handsome sum. In the parlance of economics this handsome sum was the opportunity cost of Dennis Gossen's visit.

Those opportunity costs could become very large indeed for individuals earning high incomes. As Spearman liked to tell his students, a famous lawyer who charges huge hourly fees is not the person to talk to about the weather while the lawyer's meter is running. By the same token such an attorney probably feels less able to afford a vacation than the firm's legal secretary whose opportunity costs are far lower.

The revelation of such paradoxes is what first attracted Spearman to economics. No other subject in college seemed to explain such a wide variety of human behavior so well. The psychologist could explain abnormal behavior and predict the reactions of a criminal psychopath. The sociologist endeavored to explain the folkways and mores of a mass culture. The anthropologist focused on the myths of nonliterate people. But what appealed to Spearman about economics was the economist's understanding of individuals in the ordinary business of life.

His own father illustrated the point. Spearman had never really understood his father until he studied economics. In the tailor shop that he owned, the elder Spearman was always gracious to his customers, polite and attentive to their desires. His father's reputation as a tailor was based not only upon the quality of his alterations but also his courtesy and friendliness. But when this same man climbed the flight of stairs to their brownstone tenement above the store, his disposition changed. His graciousness gave way to irritability. Within his family he had no great reputation for being attentive or concerned about the immediate desires of his wife or children. Henry Spearman could remember his mother saying, "I don't understand it, Ben, in the store you are always so nice to everyone. But the minute you get home, you become such a grouch. To Mr. Silverman, you listen to every word when he talks about his cuffs. But to me, you don't even pay attention when I talk about our own daughter's wedding dress."

Henry Spearman now had a theory that could explain his father's otherwise inexplicable behavior. It was not that his father liked Mr. Silverman more than he liked his wife and children. On the contrary, Henry knew that his father cared very much for all of his family. But the young Spearman's training in economics gave him an additional insight. His father's business was in competition with other tailor shops.

Rivalry between them was keen. Little capital in the form of money or education was needed to enter this business. And the resulting price for his father's services, while too low to make his father a rich man, was high enough to see to it that there were no long lines of unserved customers. In textbook parlance the quantity supplied equaled the quantity demanded. If there had been a queue for his father's services, he could have been rude or discriminatory to some of the customers at no economic cost to himself. But when market forces determined the price for tailoring, courtesy and service were methods for gaining and keeping customers. Rudeness and poor service, on the other hand, drove people away. The penalty for Mr. Spearman would have been reduced income.

Once Spearman understood this phenomenon, a great deal of other behavior suddenly made sense. For example, the rudeness of landlords of rent-controlled apartments where rental rates were barred by law from reaching market clearing levels; the discourtesy of butchers during World War II when the price of beef was controlled; the lack of concern on the part of other merchants during that era to the plight of customers waiting early in the morning to enter those shops lucky enough to have nylon hosiery.

Spearman was reminded of the staying power of this theory many years later when the federal government placed a lid on gasoline prices. The service station on Broadway that Spearman frequented regularly during his years in Cambridge always had treated him with civility—except during that episode. The drop in supply of gasoline that was aggravated by the price controls seemingly changed the personality of the service station's personnel. With long lines of customers all eager to pay the ceiling price, the supply of courtesy at the gas station decreased sharply. But all this changed again when the controls were lifted. Courtesy once more accompanied the transactions there.

Henry Spearman knew something that very few others would believe. And he would have been misunderstood if he expressed it openly: that his father, the gentlest of men to his customers, would behave to his family like those surly service station personnel on Broadway. It would not require a change in his father's nature. Only a change to fixed and inflexible prices.

In the family circle, where market clearing prices did not determine the allocation of resources to everyone, the elder Spearman's churlishness came at little cost. But just one floor below, in the confines of his tailor shop, the same behavior would be penalized. His father chose the disposition that suited the circumstances. And so too did the younger Spearman follow the pattern predicted by the theory. Tonight it was not a cheerful Henry Spearman who abandoned his work and prepared to attend his uninvited guest.

As Spearman trudged to his automobile in the faculty parking lot, he noticed two students walking toward him. "Good evening, Professor Spearman," said the one whose head was wrapped by a colorful scarf of Christmas red and green. As the two students approached, Spearman was able to recognize the one with the muffler as one of his graduate students.

His response to her was not as amicable as it usually was when he exchanged pleasantries with his pupils. Tonight he was more than mildly annoyed; his greeting was perfunctory. But to the student he had just acknowledged, the sign of recognition might be the high spot of her evening.

"How did you ever recognize Dr. Spearman in that outfit?"

"By the outfit."

"Huh?"

"That's the way he's been coming to class all winter. Some coats are windbreakers. His is an icebreaker. We're all tense waiting for him to arrive. Then in he comes wearing that overcoat. It's down to his ankles at one end and, with the collar up, over his ears at the other. It's purple. The buttons don't match. To top it off, he wears that brown cap with a wide, droopy brim. When he finally emerges from all that, and he gives you his cherubic smile at the start of class, you just can't be intimidated. Even though you know he's a genius."

Not only was the economist in an oversized coat, he drove an oversized car. As he eased his mauve and cerise, air-conditioned, power-steered and power-braked automobile onto Concord Avenue, he began to make his way home. His hand manipulated the lever to turn on the heater, though he knew from experience that this would prove of little avail. The drive from his office to his home was of the approximate distance required for the car's engine to warm up. Only by the time his vehicle reached the garage was the heater blowing warm air.

As Spearman drove up Concord, he saw that a note had been placed under his windshield wiper. He wished he had seen it when he first arrived at his car. His height meant that much of his driving was done looking beneath the top half of the steering wheel and just over the dashboard. The note marginally obscured the area of the windshield that was essential for his driving.

Fortunately for both Spearman and pedestrians, most of the residents of Cambridge were indoors by this time. Undergraduate students at Harvard, Radcliffe, and MIT would be eating and bantering in the commons. Less transient residents of Cambridge would be having dinner in their homes.

Many of the academicians would be having cocktails before their meals. It was a good time to be driving on what were usually congested streets. Spearman's progress was rapid. When he pulled into his garage and switched off the ignition, there was a breath of warm air emanating from the heater.

As Spearman closed the door, he reached across the hood and extracted the note from beneath the windshield wiper. As he did so, he murmured to himself, "Not my favorite way of communicating." He thought it was probably a flyer that restaurants often used in Cambridge to announce their arrival. But as he opened it, he saw it was handwritten.

The moisture on the windshield had permeated the thin paper, causing the ink to smear. In the imperfect light of the garage, it was not easily read. But as he deciphered the script, Spearman saw it was from Calvin Weber. Weber was an English professor whose specialty was Conrad. The note read,

> Pardon this litter on your windshield. I see we're fellow toilers in the P&T vineyard. Strictly entre nous, I was sorry to see Foster Barrett on Clegg's list. Good to know you're on board. Calvin Weber.

Spearman stuffed the note into his overcoat pocket. He too was pleased. Calvin Weber was one of his and Pidge's favorites. But, busy beavers both, they had been unable to get together for some time.

A half-smile crossed Spearman's lips. Weber's unease about Barrett was probably more than matched by Barrett's unease about Weber, the economist thought. Weber was the son of a Mississippi sharecropper. He had been educated at Tougaloo and Howard. This was hardly the background, either familial or academic, that Barrett found suitable for Harvard. Barrett, courtly and polite, would manifest his disapproval in subtle ways. But not too subtle to escape the notice of Calvin Weber.

Spearman's thoughts turned to the event that had brought him home. He left the garage and entered the back door of his house. He was already annoyed at his junior colleague, and his facial expression did little to conceal this.

"Hello, Henry," Pidge said, greeting him at the door. "Was there much traffic on the way home?"

"No, the roads are fine," her husband replied. "Is our guest in the living room?"

"Yes, he is. I thought you'd want to talk in your study, but I didn't take him in there."

"Well, why don't you go to Sage's before it gets any later, if you like. I'll see what Mr. Gossen wants." Henry Spearman was taking off his wraps.

"Don't be angry with him, Henry. He seems very anxious about something." Pidge gathered her coat and purse and made her way out the back door. At the same time Henry Spearman headed for the dining room, which opened into the large living room of the Spearmans' home. There, on the Queen Anne sofa, facing the front window, was Dennis Gossen, who nervously rose as his senior colleague entered.

"Prof—, I mean Henry. I'm sorry to call you back from Littauer. But I felt it was very important to see you." Whether to call full professors by their first names or address them by their last was an eternal struggle for an assistant professor in the Ivy League. With some members of the senior faculty, the matter was clear. They were so aloof that only the use of the title fit. But others let it be known that their view of collegial behavior put everyone on a first-name basis. With Spearman, the decision was unclear. He had a reputation for accessibility and good-natured humor. And he was rarely stern, even when dealing with less diligent students. But he was definitely not one of the guys. His reputation in the economics profession would always preclude that.

"Sit down, Dennis. I see my wife offered you some tea. What is it that I might help you with?"

"It involves my promotion. I believe . . ."

Spearman interrupted him bluntly, almost physically. "You know I cannot discuss that with you. The P and T deliberations have begun, and I think you are aware that members are to have no contact with candidates."

"But I'm not trying to curry your favor as a committee member. I need your advice on a very delicate matter."

"Does it in any way bear on your promotion?"

"Well, yes, it could, but . . ."

"If that's the case, then we simply must terminate our discussion."

Thwarted by the older economist's implacability, Gossen tried one more time. "If you would just hear me out . . ." His eyes implored his senior colleague.

But Spearman would not budge. "I'm sorry, I'm sorry, Dennis, there is no point in your being stubborn about this matter. I will not hear you." He was waving his hands before him as he spoke, in the manner one would use to stop an oncoming car. Then Spearman, never having settled into a chair, at this point left the living room to retrieve Gossen's coat and hat from their place on the kitchen table. The frustrated young economist found himself being helped into his coat and firmly ushered out the front door.

Gossen hesitated on the front porch, uncertain of his next move. He knew that reopening a dialogue with Henry Spearman was impossible. The young professor looked up and down Appleton Street. The soft lights from the faculty homes glowed invitingly. But they did nothing to ease the feeling of rejection. Still, Gossen was not yet at the end of his tether. His first option had proved inaccessible. Now he was left with the less attractive alternatives. And if his efforts were to prove in vain, there was a remaining trump card he hoped he would never have to play.

4
Friday, December 21

Oliver Wu, as the saying goes, did not suffer fools gladly. And tonight he was anything but glad. His task for the evening was evaluating candidates for promotion at Harvard. As he scanned an article from the file of Dennis Gossen, he sat immobile, like a sculptured Egyptian cat, moving nothing but his dark eyes behind their walls of glass. Cataract operations had years ago forced him into spectacles with lenses like Coke bottle bottoms, and they gave his countenance an owl-like, peering quality. His black, glistening hair was combed straight back and his face was punctuated by a closely trimmed mustache.

Wu was a man of strong views. As a sociologist his name was preeminently associated with criminology, though he never chose to use the word criminologist to describe himself. Outside the United States, the field of criminology was dominated largely by psychiatrists who saw the cause of crime as being pathological in nature. Wu, along with other sociologists, recognized the influence of cultural and social factors in criminal conduct.

Wu's formal academic training in the study of crime had been in the Continental tradition where scholars, following Lombroso, believed there was a criminal type, potentially identifiable by biological or even anatomical characteristics. When Wu came to the United States and became acquainted with the writings of Edwin H. Sutherland, he had an experience akin to Saint Paul's on the road to Damascus.

Sutherland was unabashedly a sociological criminologist. Over the course of two decades, Wu's own writings had powerfully influenced the course of criminology, as he took Sutherland's lead to develop his own theory of the multidimensional nature of criminal behavior. Moreover, he had assembled large data sets on many characteristics and facets of criminal behavior. Any scholar who attempted to reduce the complexity of criminal activity to a single cause was regarded by Wu not only with suspicion but with contempt.

Wu pushed back the Windsor chair at his carrel and purposefully walked through the gray metal shelves in Harvard's Widener library. Unlike many of his colleagues, who had established spacious and even elaborate studies in their homes, Wu did much of his work at this location. His office in William James Hall was a place to converse with his students and his faculty colleagues, but he considered it hopeless to do concentrated reading there. The place to get real work done, Wu insisted, was at a carrel in the bowels of a good library. But Wu's preferences went even deeper. He loved everything about the stacks: their fusty aroma, their cavernous silence, and the sense of isolation. To a man of Wu's disposition, the stacks were a refuge from the hurly-burly of the world's commerce as well as a repository of the world's knowledge.

A quarter-hour later, his foray completed, Wu returned to his carrel with a gray, medium-thick volume he had taken from its place in the stacks. He shifted back into his chair as he placed the book next to the Gossen file, which had on top of it the last reprint Wu had read in evaluating the young scholar's work. Wu had perceived that the economist was a modern version of Jeremy Bentham, who had written on crime and punishment a century and a half before. Bentham was the father of utilitarianism, which judged all laws and actions by whether on balance they augmented the happiness of the community or diminished it. To Bentham, human beings were seen to be in a constant process of judging and evaluating. Wu had found it convenient to use Bentham in his classroom as the exemplar of a long-since-discarded, unidimensional view of human nature.

Before modern sociology had revealed its deficiencies, Bentham's was the accepted view of how human beings behaved. But Wu's students in sociology were generally unaware that a view of man as single-minded calculator once held sway. So Wu found it useful to quote Bentham directly from the text in order to convince his students that their professor was not contrasting modern sociology with a straw man.

Wu now felt it advisable to come equipped on January 8th with the evidence that not only was there once someone who thought this way, but that one hundred and fifty years later a candidate for promotion at Harvard was using this same antiquated view of human nature as the basis of scholarly argument.

Wu flipped through the pages of the cumbersomely titled volume. He knew what he was looking for and where it was. At page 188 he found the quotation, which he began to copy into his notes. ". . . who is there that does not calculate? Men calculate, some with less exactness, indeed, some with more: but all men calculate." No one in criminology denied that individuals calculated. What Wu found so repugnant and absurd in the work of Gossen that he had just read was the overarching principle that people *only* calculated.

The Gossen article that had miffed Wu, and which Wu now filed away as he prepared to leave Widener, was entitled

"Wage Differentials and Malefaction." It was a short piece, as articles in scholarly journals go, chock-full of figures on the wages of purchasing agents, those who selected the inputs of a business enterprise. Gossen had gathered data on the wages of these employees and had found that agents who were in the employ of businesses that were growing faster and had more faddish and seasonal products were more highly paid than comparably trained and educated purchasing agents in more stable industries. For example, purchasing agents who bought high-fashion clothes were paid more than ones who bought machine tools.

The theory or explanation the young economist was testing, and which he claimed to find vindicated, concerned the deterrence of malefaction. In markets where it was more difficult to monitor the skill and integrity of a purchasing agent, such as the buyer for a ready-to-wear chain, the rational employer paid the rational employee a higher wage. This was to help ensure that the employee, if tempted by a bribe from a particular clothing manufacturer, would be more tempted by the higher salary to operate in the best interests of his or her employer, turning down the bribe and not buying less desirable merchandise. The purchasing agent in the stodgier market, whose malefaction would be more easily detected by the employer, need not be so generously compensated to remain honest. In Gossen's theory it was not that honest people are paid more because of their honesty. Rather they are paid more in order to make them more honest. To Oliver Wu this seemed quite foolish.

Wu closed his briefcase on the Gossen file and the publications of the other candidates he had been studying that day. He straightened the books used in his own research that he would leave at his carrel and made his way out of the

Widener stacks. Each day at 7:00 p.m., unless he had called the livery company with contrary instructions, he was met by a taxicab at Harvard Square to take him home. His eyes did not permit him to drive.

As Oliver Wu prepared to leave the library, he tried to place himself in a world of pure costs and benefits, where people responded to prices but not values—the people who inhabited the theories of Dennis Gossen.

He approached the desk at the front door of Widener. Should he steal a book? The thought had not, to his conscious knowledge, occurred to him before. What were the costs? The monitor at the door might detect his attempt at theft, which would prove embarrassing. But not deeply so, since his explanation of absentmindedness would be readily accepted by the attendant. Wu had, after all, exited from Widener literally hundreds of times and the chances of his even being checked were less than 50–50. Then there were the pangs of conscience that he might suffer as a result of his transgression. Stealing was considered highly sinful within the family circle in which he was raised. His values were of the old world, and he knew that his remorse for violating such a strongly held taboo would not be de minimus. Then there was the cost of lugging a heavy volume home. He was not used to physical exertion. Next he estimated the cost of storing the book and occasionally dusting it. Where does this cost-counting stop, he puzzled. When the cost of counting the cost is too costly?

Wu then turned his imagination to the benefits side of the equation. The gains seemed small. There was of course the benefit of the information contained in the book and possibly the pleasure of reading it. But this was available to him already, through the collection at Widener, and for him at little trouble since he frequented his favorite sanctuary so often. He could of course sell the book for cash. But a volume that bore the stamped identity of a library book would bring little in the market. He could think of no other benefits. In his decision calculus the costs clearly outweighed the benefits. Wu supposed that Gossen would have him not steal the book.

Leaving the library, the distinguished sociologist made his way down the stone stairs into the cold air of the early evening. The walks of Harvard Yard had been shoveled clear; snow was piled high bordering the concrete pathways. He proceeded south beside the building to Massachusetts Avenue which he crossed over to reach his cabstand at the Square. His cab was waiting for him.

"Hello, Dr. Wu. Want to go straight home tonight?"

"Is that you, Raymond?" Wu inquired, peering through his thick spectacles. Recognizing the driver as one who often carried him home, Wu entered the back door of the well-worn Chevrolet and placed his briefcase on the black, vinyl seat.

"Yes, let's go straight home," he directed.

As the cab made its way up Brattle Street toward Wu's home, his thoughts were jarred by the blaring of a horn from the rear. From the front seat, Wu heard Raymond curse quietly to himself as he wheeled the taxi close to the side of the road to let the speeding automobile pass.

Aggressive driving was a common tactic in the Greater Boston area. But it was typically acted out through daring behavior at intersections and in navigating narrow streets. The speed of the sedan that passed Wu's cab was unusual by any standard.

"That guy's in a hurry for his own funeral," Raymond said as the sedan raced by.

In spite of himself, Wu's thoughts turned once again to

Bentham. And to calculation. A Benthamite would argue that the decision to speed made by the driver of the blue sedan was done by balancing the inconvenience of missing an appointment against the possibility of being apprehended by the police and convicted of violating the law. There could be a fine imposed, and if the speeding led to injury or even death, the penalty could be far worse. On balance the driver had chosen to speed rather than obey the law because the net benefits came out ahead of the costs. The seemingly irrational act of reckless driving, Wu realized, could be construed as nothing more than a rational response to cost-benefit calculation. Indeed, to a person of Gossen's mentality, Wu reflected, the entire criminal code would be simply a price list for various acts. It is as if all of us, as individuals, are confronted with an elaborate menu. Should you overpark? Look at the price and make your choice. You will overpark only if the inconvenience of moving your car is greater than the cost of the fine. And you are fined only if you are caught in the act—which may not happen. What are the chances of being caught? That has to be calculated also.

The querulousness that enshrouded Wu earlier was beginning to fade. He was enjoying this game in a perverse kind of way. Wu toyed with other items on the menu: the costs and benefits of cheating on his income tax, of padding his travel expenses to an academic meeting. Then a diabolical thought crossed his mind. What about murder? Is that a selection on the menu? Why not? Should I commit murder? The great driving power of his ambition combined with his persistence and intelligence had led him to his present position of prominence. But there had been great disappointments along the way, not, he believed, because of his failings but because of the connivings of others.

Now he was sunk deep in thought. Not all murderers are caught. That possibility must, as Gossen would have put it, "be discounted" by an appropriate calculation. And even if apprehended, there is some calculable possibility of escaping conviction. And then there were the sizable benefits to be considered.

Wu's eyes were half closed behind the heavy eyeglasses. He shifted his gaze from the traffic. Through the closed windows of the cab he could barely make out the distant banging of a clock as it chimed out the quarter-hour. He felt deeply uneasy. His thoughts had taken a direction he had not anticipated when he first began to reflect on the economic perspective of crime. But the play of unremitting self-interested calculation had proved too compelling. The barriers had fallen. In his imagination he suddenly saw the face of his greatest enemy, the one person he hated most of all in this world. Rapid-fire calculations raced through his brain. Then his mind rested. In the game he was playing, Wu had discovered the fatal equilibrium.

5
Saturday, December 22

"I didn't even hear you come in last night. And I was up till quite late." Pidge Spearman was slicing oranges at the drainboard of their spacious kitchen.

"It was late, mom. The roads were bad coming from Philadelphia and I didn't make the best of time. But dad was still up and let me in. You know, I don't think I have a key to the house anymore." Patricia Spearman went to the sink to help her mother prepare breakfast.

"Well, your father and I are glad you can be home for the holidays. He'll be down in a minute. Would you finish making the coffee?" Pidge Spearman motioned to the percolator.

"Dad was up late last night, too," Patricia said, as she responded to her mother's request. "He had his stamp collection out. I haven't seen him with that in so long. He said something about how his evening had not gone well, so he could afford to work on his stamps."

At that moment Henry Spearman entered the room. "Can I help with anything?" he said cheerily.

"We're just about ready to eat," Pidge replied, as the Spearman family, no longer often united, prepared to sit down to a New England breakfast of hotcakes and Vermont maple syrup.

Breakfasts at the Spearman household were still old-fashioned. Frozen juice concentrate, pancake mixes, ersatz maple syrup, and freeze-dried coffee were not for Pidge Spearman.

In her home everything was "from scratch," as she liked to say. Pidge Spearman was a firm believer in a robust breakfast to begin the day. In earlier years she would no more have let Patricia leave the house on a wintry day without a breakfast of hot cereal or pancakes or eggs and freshly baked bread than she would have allowed her daughter to leave without a coat and gloves.

"So, is the demand for veterinary services increasing?" Henry Spearman asked, as his fork cut through a stack of flapjacks. Patricia Spearman, after completing studies in veterinary medicine at Cornell, had begun her practice in Philadelphia less than two years ago.

"I don't know if it is increasing or not. But I'm so busy that sometimes I wonder if I'll get though the day. That's why it's great to be home for a few days with no ailing animals to see. And not being on call at the zoo—that's a luxury."

"If you are busier than you want," Henry Spearman said, "there's an obvious solution to that. Simply raise your rates," Spearman said between mouthfuls.

"Dad, if I raised my rates, I think I'd have even more business. Some people in Philadelphia pick their vets based on their rates. They want to go to the highest priced ones."

Henry Spearman found this conversational morsel more tempting than the breakfast in front of him. But before he could reply, Pidge, who knew from years of experience when an economics lecture was forthcoming, looked for a diversion.

"Patty, when you were home last summer you said that you had pulled a tooth from an elephant. Do you ever see that animal anymore?"

"Oh, that was Ike, mom, the zoo's African elephant. He's an example of why I love my work at the zoo. Ike had a toothache last July, so we had to operate to extract the tooth and clear up an infection. In Ike's mind, he associates me with the relief from this pain. Everytime I go to the zoo, he prances over to see me like a little puppy."

"A little puppy indeed! Be careful you're not trampled," Pidge exhorted between sips from her cup of freshly perked coffee.

Both Pidge and her husband were duly proud of their daughter's professional accomplishments. Nowadays, gaining entrance into veterinary school was more difficult than going to medical school. In fact, had their daughter not been accepted into a school of veterinary medicine, she would have become a physician. But her undergraduate record had secured for her positive responses at both Cornell and Michigan State. Her desire to be closer to home had made the choice easier.

"I can picture you caring for dogs and cats," Pidge Spearman continued, "but when you go to the zoo. . . I somehow can't imagine you operating on a lion or pulling the tooth from an elephant."

"But mom, large animals are my first love. And I feel fortunate to be on call at the zoo at this stage of my career."

"On call at the zoo?" asked her father. "People doctors long ago gave up making house calls. Their customers come to them. Why do you make cage calls?"

Patricia Spearman immediately saw that for once the shoe was on the other foot. She would not miss her opportunity. "Why it's simply a matter of economics, dad."

Henry Spearman winced. He was unaccustomed to having some fine point of economics explained to him, especially in his own family. He looked expectantly at his daughter. "Economics? What economic principle would cause veterinarians to behave differently from physicians?"

"The law of demand. You always said that was the most

basic law in economics. Well, can you imagine what it would do to the quantity demanded in my practice if there was a gorilla sitting in my waiting room?" Spearman affected a pained expression on his face in the manner of one who had just heard a corny pun. Pidge and Patricia were enjoying his reaction and Spearman did not want to spoil their fun.

For this reason he refrained from telling them that part of his exasperated look was triggered by his daughter's error. She had confused "demand" with "quantity demanded." A serious gaffe for an economist but not for a veterinarian, he mused. Spearman was tempted to explain the difference. but even more tempting was Pidge's offer of a second helping of flapjacks. Between the two choices even the didactic professor did not hesitate.

6
Saturday, December 22

Patricia Spearman's bright red Rabbit crossed the Charles as she and her father traveled to Boston on the shopping excursion they had planned the night before. The young veterinarian intended to buy holiday gifts for her parents, and Professor Spearman welcomed the opportunity to accompany his daughter and make a purchase himself.

"Shall we make Filene's our first stop?" Patricia asked as they made their way up Cambridge Street into the city.

"That would be fine. From there we can go over to Bromfield Street where I'd like to end up. I want to visit a shop there."

Patricia drove her car into a parking garage, locked the vehicle, and with her father headed for the exit. Walking up Washington Street to Boston's most celebrated department store, the two Spearmans were further engaged in getting up to date on each other's recent activities. Neither was a particularly systematic correspondent. Henry Spearman explained his current time-intensive commitment to Harvard's promotion and tenure committee and his forthcoming trip to London. Patricia talked about the friends she had made in Philadelphia, her new apartment, and the conference of zoo veterinarians she was planning to attend in Florida next summer. Though heartily engaged in conversation, they could not be oblivious to others, for the Christmas shopping rush in Boston was nearing its peak. The sidewalks and stores were packed with people.

As the couple entered Filene's, Patricia expressed her preference to shop alone. "You understand, dad, I want what I buy to be a surprise. Why don't we meet at the Washington Street entrance in an hour? Will that be too long?"

"At 11:00, then," Henry Spearman replied. "That will give me ample time to browse."

Notwithstanding the high value Henry Spearman placed upon his time, he did not consider "browsing," as he put it, a wasteful or purposeless activity. For he believed deeply that while economic analysis applied to all nooks and crannies of the human experience, it shone most brilliantly in its treatment and investigation of the world of commerce. Alfred Marshall, the English economist whom Spearman ranked over even John Maynard Keynes as the preeminent twentieth-century thinker, had described economics as "the study of mankind in the ordinary business of life." On December 22nd, in any American city, shopping at a department store was most certainly ordinary business.

But what Spearman found not so ordinary at Filene's was their basement floor and the pricing of the merchandise to be found there. It was a system that brought into play all of the subtle forces of human ingenuity, utility-maximizing, and profit-seeking that to Spearman made a market-organized economy so engaging.

Spearman left the decorum of Filene's first floor and embarked on the escalator to the basement. Even before he could see the mass of shoppers and mounds of merchandise, he detected the hubbub that was so characteristic of this portion of the store. And at this time of year the ruckus was only raised to a higher degree.

"It's mine. I had it first!"

"No way, buddy. I've been eyeing this for two weeks."

As he stepped off the escalator, Spearman turned his head in the direction of the contretemps. Two young men each had hold of a sleeve of the same tweed sport jacket. A tug-of-war had now supplanted their verbal dispute. Suddenly the shyer of the two relinquished his grip and gave up the struggle, while the victor hastened to the cash register to claim his spoils. What would have been considered a shocking display of ill manners on any other floor of Filene's, here attracted no attention, save for that of the balding professor, who reflected on the deeper significance of it all.

Lincoln Filene, for many years the guiding genius behind the department store, had long ago instituted a pricing system in the basement of his downtown Boston establishment which differed from that used in the rest of the store. At the lower level merchandise was offered on sale. But the reduction was not simply a given percentage off a list price. The discount was a moving one, systematic and predictable in its direction and magnitude. All merchandise in the basement was first marked with a sale price. But these prices were marked down twenty-five percent every week. The merchandise remained in the store no more than four weeks, at which time it was at the rock-bottom sale price. For any item not sold by that time, it was the policy of Filene's to donate it to charity.

Quite apart from the moving discount, Filene's was not a typical bargain basement where the items sold for less simply because the quality was inferior. Quite the opposite. In Filene's basement was merchandise that earlier had graced the racks and shelves of some of the most fashionable departments on the floors above. In addition, it was common to find other items bearing the labels of some of the most prestigious department stores in America.

Every knowledgeable customer was aware that over time,

within the thirty-day limit, an item would become cheaper each week. But what could not be predicted was whether there was some other shopper who was also surveying the item and who would buy it before the price reached its low point. Up to a limit, there was an incentive to wait. But in waiting, many disappointed customers learned, one ran the risk of losing the item altogether. On the other hand, buying too soon was to forgo the possibility of future savings on the same item. The customer in Filene's basement walked the razor's edge between buying too soon and waiting too long.

Spearman immediately recognized this predicament as one he had experienced himself when attending a Dutch auction. He had been in the Netherlands to give a series of lectures. His hosts, knowing his interest in market behavior, had taken him to the town of Aalsmeer where he had witnessed the sale of tulip bulbs. What was amazing to Spearman was the fact that the Dutch auction was topsy-turvy. It was conducted in reverse. What he had been used to was the typical auction in the New England countryside, the kind that he and Pidge had enjoyed attending on warm, weekend afternoons. The auctioneer always began the bidding at a low price—one that many in attendance would have jumped at paying—but the bidding escalated until there was only one bidder.

In Holland, however, everything about the procedure was backward. There was no auctioneer rhythmically chanting the prices. Instead the initial price was registered on the face of what appeared to be a clock. But it wasn't really a clock. The numbers on its face did not denote time; they represented prices. And there was one hand, not two. That single hand swept systematically to lower prices—until a buyer, with the push of a button, stopped the clock. The first person to do this purchased the merchandise.

The parallel between the Dutch auction and Filene's basement was exact. Just as the animated, frenetic buyer in Filene's knew that waiting too long would mean going without, so the stolid, impassive Dutch burgher knew that at any moment the tulip bulbs on the block might not be his if he tarried too long.

Bumped hard, Spearman felt his balance go. One of Filene's larger and more aggressive customers—like a bull running through the streets of Pamplona—had butted the diminutive economist. The forward momentum landed him in a rack of bathrobes. Henry Spearman tried to grab the pipe on which the robes hung, but missed. Losing his footing, he landed first against and then beneath the dangling terrycloth. Peering out from between the soft cotton garments, he detected the pants and hosiery of customers who occupied the aisle from which he had just been ejected. The department store's bedlam continued unabated.

Henry Spearman crawled out from under the bathrobes and with his index finger pushed the bridge of his glasses back into place. After he righted himself and dusted off his coat sleeves and trousers, he inspected for bruises. Of physical bruises, there were none. Still, his ego was damaged, obvious from the blush in his cheeks. He preferred to be in control. The pratfall had embarrassed him and he decided to make an exit from the hazards of the bargain basement. It would be less risky to observe shoppers' behavior in the appliance department.

"It helps to be streetwise when you shop here, Henry."

Spearman was stopped in his retreat to the escalator by a familiar voice. He turned around and was surprised to see Calvin Weber, whose eyes gleamed with amusement.

"It also helps to be six feet three," Spearman replied. His

face broke into a grin. "What are you doing here? I suspect it's not to watch markets equilibrate."

"No, but I did see my favorite economist in a rare state of disequilibrium. That guy gave you quite a wallop."

"Well, I confess I did get something more than I bargained for in the bargain basement. By the way, thanks for the note you left for me yesterday. I was pleased to see that Denton put you on the P and T committee as well. Apart from Denton and you, I hardly know any of the others."

"Oh, it's quite a crew. One of the Dean's better balancing acts. Ethnically, racially, sexually, and departmentally—he's covered all the bases."

"Denton is a master at that," Spearman responded. "When he was first appointed dean, I thought, what a waste of scholarly talent. But his talent as a dean matches his talent as a scholar. Every other dean I've known has had to put research on the back burner, at least partially. But Denton somehow forges ahead on both fronts."

"I've no reservations about Clegg as an administrator. I simply think he's naive. He continues to commit the naturalistic fallacy when he puts together faculty. In the case of our committee, he thinks that if Foster Barrett and I have to work together, we'll come to overlook our differences. But Barrett's a bigot and I'm a black. Juxtaposition on the P and T committee won't change that."

"I wouldn't call Barrett a bigot," Spearman replied. "A snob he is. No doubt about that. Social position counts with him. But he's known as a decent scholar, and he cares about the university. He only wishes his colleagues had better table manners."

"You're right, Henry. Barrett has no objection whatsoever to dark skin, as long as it's a summer tan from the Cape."

"It isn't a matter of skin pigment," Spearman said. "Foster Barrett's tastes are to associate with the first families of Boston. The fact that neither you nor I fall into that category means that we are not going to be invited to his home for dinner. But there is no reason to believe that this taste extends to professional associations."

"Henry, we've been round this point before. I don't know whether to be impressed or appalled by your unflagging tolerance. Marcuse spoke of repressive tolerance, meaning there are times when tolerance itself should not be tolerated. I have sympathy with that idea."

"But Marcuse never explained how we decide precisely who is too intolerant. I'll take my chances with the Barretts of the world rather than a government's intolerance committee. It is the age-old question, Calvin: *Quis custodiet ipsos custodet?*" The noisiness of the Filene's bazaar continued as the two friends strained to hear each other above the din. It was Calvin Weber who attempted to bring the conversation down from its lofty plane.

"What are you shopping for, Henry? I know you didn't come for the pleasure of being bowled over by the crazies— like me—who are regulars here."

"Actually, I didn't come down here to buy anything. I wanted to watch those who were. I was enjoying the scene, even making some mental notes about consumer surplus, when I got hit from behind. Hardly the usual occupational hazard for an economist."

"You were blind-sided, my friend, take it from an over-the-hill football player. Actually, when I come here, my days as a tight end are very helpful." Weber's curiosity then got the best of him. "Do you actually come here often just to watch people shop?"

"Not often, but whenever I do, it is instructive. For example, it occurred to me today that the Filene's bargain basement system is ingeniously devised to extract the maximum of what Alfred Marshall called 'consumer surplus.' "

"Consumer surplus? I doubt if I get much of that, on an English professor's salary." Weber made a pretense at being interested in his friend's economic disquisition.

"I must differ with you there, Calvin. Take the ball-point pen in your shirt pocket. How much did you pay for it?"

Weber looked down at the green and white plastic tube clipped in his pocket. "Fifty cents," he hazarded.

The economist pointed his index finger upward toward Weber's face. "Right, but did you know that when Milton Reynolds invented the ball-point pen after World War II and had a monopoly on its production, he sold them for as much as eighteen dollars each? Now there are many producers of ball-point pens, and you pay no more than fifty cents to get one. Maybe you wouldn't have been one of those willing to pay as much as eighteen dollars, not even sixteen dollars. But I'll bet you would have been willing to pay a good deal more than fifty cents in order to have the convenience of a ball point instead of a fountain pen. Whatever that difference is, is your consumer surplus. And make no mistake about it, Calvin, you're getting consumer surplus all over the place. In a competitive economy people usually pay for most items far less than the amount they would be willing to pay rather than go without them. That difference is Marshall's consumer surplus. Whoever dreamt up Filene's bargain basement put the concept into very profitable practice."

"How is that?" Weber was now curious, in spite of himself, for Spearman's enthusiasm was infectious.

"By extracting as much of it as possible for Filene's. As you know, in a regular auction you always have a last chance to bid on any item that you dearly want. If other bidders don't want the item, you can get it with a low bid after they have dropped out. Your consumer surplus then might be large. But Filene's basement is like a Dutch auction. If a buyer here tries too hard to maximize consumer surplus, he runs the risk of losing the item completely. The tendency for a person strongly attracted to an item is to be the first to bid on it, forgoing possible consumer surplus gains by waiting."

"C'mon, Henry, do you think the management here read Marshall?"

"Probably not—though Marshall had hoped that business managers would be the main customers for his book. But ingenious managers over and over devise business practices by intuition, practices that economists come to understand only years later." The professor was now leaning against the side of the escalator, his arms folded across his chest. He was in a state of repose. It was clear to Weber that the economics lecture had ended.

Calvin Weber decided not to take any chances that a new one would commence. Instead he shifted the theme of the conversation. "By the way, have you done all your homework for the January 8th meeting?"

"I picked up the last batch yesterday. I could barely make my way back to Littauer with it. There's a lot to read and some of it is tough sledding, but I hope to be ready by then. How goes the assignment for you?"

"You may remember, I've got a reduced teaching load this semester. Not having exams to grade has been great for reading the promotion files. I took the subway in this morning for a break. I want to check out some sport coats for me and my son, then get back to P and T files."

"Well, if you're planning to do some more shopping down here, remember, Calvin, don't let Filene's extract too much of your consumer surplus. All it takes on your part is a little nerve, a little patience, and a willingness to risk going without once in awhile." With that, Spearman turned, grasped the moving bannister, and made his way to the first floor.

7
Saturday, December 22

The great American department store was like a giant cupboard that never went bare, in spite of the efforts of thousands who daily tried to empty it of its bounty. And their efforts were especially tenacious during the Christmas shopping season. The flood of traffic at its portals streamed energetically both in and out of the store, the way a riptide runs in opposite directions at the same time.

Henry Spearman was a part of and yet apart from the crowd. A part of the crowd, because he too was a shopper at this holiday season, doing his bit to add to the commotion; but apart from the crowd because Henry Spearman was a detached observer of the scene. A detached observer who was now having trouble observing—as he waited at the Washington Street entrance for his daughter.

He heard her voice before he saw her. Or at least he thought it was her voice. He could not be sure until she pushed past a batch of package-laden customers who had obstructed his view. "I hope you haven't been waiting too long. I'm afraid I lost track of time."

"Not at all. I'm glad you're late because I just got here myself. I ran into Calvin Weber—you remember him, don't you?—and we got to exchanging small talk. I didn't have a chance to pick up the item I want to get here. Do you know where housewares is located?"

"Yes, I came by there on my way down."

"Then lead the way, Patricia. I have something in mind for your mother."

Patricia expertly negotiated her way through the crowds, her father in tow. The certain knowledge of the location of the housewares department gave her an advantage in speed over the less informed. As he followed his daughter, Henry Spearman thought that efforts to find an item often took up more of a shopper's time than that needed to make a purchase once the item was located. Another example of the value of information. Patricia's knowledge of the location of an otherwise elusive product would reduce his search costs, Spearman realized.

"Have you been waited on?" a clerk, already harried from the morning's activities, inquired.

"May I see your paring knives?"

The clerk pointed. "They are over against that wall."

A display of cutlery was arrayed on the east partition of the housewares department. The clerk led him in the direction of the merchandise. The inventory ranged from tiny scoops for slicing melon balls to cleavers large enough to split bone and gristle in a butcher shop. Henry Spearman's preference was for a less specialized implement.

"I noticed your mother struggling to slice those oranges this morning. That paring knife she was using is one she's had for years. I want to get her a nice new one."

"A new paring knife, how dashing and romantic," Patricia teased her father. "Make sure you have it gift wrapped with a beautiful bow. Mom might expect a bracelet in a box that size. Especially if it's beautifully wrapped. Imagine her delight when she finds it's a paring knife instead."

"I think I'll leave off the bow in deference to Adam Smith, who set the romantic level for all economists ever after. Smith said, 'I'm a beau in nothing but my books.' For romance, far better a paring knife than a bracelet." Spearman looked at his daughter impishly, watching for her reaction. "Does that surprise you? It shouldn't, Patty. Romance takes time; sharp paring knives save time. Did you notice how long it took your mother to slice those oranges this morning? A bracelet wouldn't have made the task go any faster. But a new paring knife might save her an average of five minutes a day, or possibly a half hour a week. That's a half hour for romance that we wouldn't have if I'd given her a new bracelet but left her with an old paring knife."

He acted decisively. "Would you gift wrap this, please?" He handed to the clerk a paring knife that he had selected from the assortment before him. Spearman glanced at the price tag attached to the implement. "That would be $8.32 with tax, is that correct?" he inquired as he reached into his pocket.

"Doesn't that seem steep for a paring knife? I think if you searched around a bit, you could do better." Patricia Spearman raised her eyebrows in an inquiring expression.

"I have no doubt at all that if I spent the rest of the day shopping for paring knives, I'd probably find a much lower price than this one. But you've got to consider the value of time. Shopping for paring knives is not my idea of the best way to spend my day."

"That seems inconsistent with what you told me on the way into town this morning."

"Which was. . . ?"

"That you were taking off all day Monday to shop for a new car."

"But why is that inconsistent with my not shopping all day for a paring knife?"

"Because of what you said about the value of time. It seems to me that a day spent shopping for an automobile takes as much time as a day spent searching for a paring knife."

"Of course that's true, Patty. But if I find an unusually good deal on a car as a result of a diligent search, it will be worth the time spent compared to my getting a better deal on a paring knife. Just think of the savings at the end of the day. That's why an individual searches much longer for a big ticket item—like an automobile—than for a small ticket item like a paring knife. At *some* point of course, a person will decide that it's not worth going to another auto dealer, for the same reason that I decided, just now, not to visit another housewares department or hardware store—even though I suspect I'd eventually find a lower price by doing so."

The young clerk, looking as harried as before, returned with the Spearman purchase. "Here you are, sir—all wrapped and ready to go."

Taking the package in hand, Henry Spearman adjusted his all-enveloping purple chesterfield in preparation for the outdoor weather. "Patricia, if you'd be so good as to run interference out of here, we'll make our way to Bromfield Street."

Bromfield Street in Boston was once one of the great marketplaces for stamps. In an earlier day several merchants occupied storefronts on the street, and philatelists in considerable number were drawn by the enormous inventory of stamps offered by these dealers as well as the information they had about the whereabouts and values of other stamps they did not themselves stock. Bromfield Street also had been a geographic focal point for gossip and camaraderie among serious philatelists. Shopping malls had caused a dispersion of markets and Bromfield Street was no longer the center it once was. But it was still the address of several established dealers.

The Spearmans stood before a varnished oak door set into a tiny vestibule that fronted on Bromfield Street. The portal to the vestibule was guarded by a sliding iron security grate, which was now collapsed like a closed accordion against the side post. An oval window on the door had in Gothic print the name "Burckhardt" printed across its center. Pausing for a moment to collect his thoughts, the way serious shoppers generally do, Henry Spearman escorted his daughter into the establishment.

"This should take only a few minutes, Patricia. I know exactly what I want here." They crossed a floor tiled in the pattern of small white octagons and approached a glass-topped display case. The fruitwood frame of the case's top was worn and rounded by the hands of thousands of stamp collectors who in the course of their dealings had smoothly sanded the surface and brought out the cabinet's intricate graining. An elderly clerk, whose stoop gave him the posture of a question mark, waited behind the counter. In back of him, from the floor to the ceiling, were shelves containing large morocco-bound volumes of stamp albums, the names of the territories they encompassed embossed in gold leaf on the spines; catalogs containing the descriptions and prices of postage stamps—Scott's, Gibbon's, and Minkus—were stacked along the shelves and available for sale. Copies of these catalogs also were on the counters ready for easy reference by customers and clerks.

"May I help you, sir?" the salesman inquired softly.

"I was in several days ago and spoke with Mr. Burckhardt about a 'United States Black Jack.' I've decided to purchase it. I believe in your stock it is number 118-A."

"A wonderful investment," the clerk replied with an equanimity honed by years of experience. "Are you collecting American Presidents?"

"Actually no. My interest is former French colonies in Africa. This is for a close friend."

"Aren't you adding this to your own collection?" Patricia asked.

"No, this particular stamp is a present for Denton Clegg. It's a black stamp with a wonderful engraving of Andrew Jackson. Your mother and I are giving a small dinner party for the Cleggs in a few days. It's Denton's sixtieth birthday and tenth year as dean. You know that he loves philately. And Jessica assures me that the stamp will complete an important part of his collection. I wanted something special to mark the occasion."

"Ah, Dr. Spearman, have you come to a decision about the Black Jack?" Henry Spearman turned around to face Christolph Burckhardt, the proprietor and the doyen of philately on the East Coast. For thirty-five years, ever since he had come to the United States from Geneva, Burckhardt had bought and sold stamps from this same storefront location. His fame rested upon his having held in his stock at one time or another every great stamp known in the philatelic world. He bought and sold these rarities as an agent for wealthy collectors and on their behalf was a frequent visitor to the great auction rooms whenever any of the stamps went on the block. Connoisseurs of stamps knew that in dealing with Christolph Burckhardt one had an agent who combined both the aplomb and the discretion associated with a Swiss diplomat. His expertise was sought after—as an appraiser of a stamp's present worth and as a predictor of its future value. Whenever one of the truly famous stamps came into his possession, between its purchase and delivery to his usually anonymous customers, that item was shown in the small display window facing Bromfield Street.

"Yes, I've already placed the order with your clerk. Thank you for your kindness in discussing the stamp with me." Spearman knew that his purchase was a modest one, light-years away in fame and value from the 1856 British Guiana one-cent black-on-magenta Burckhardt had recently brokered. But they both were aware that the bread and butter of any stamp dealer was just the kind of purchase that Spearman was making. The rarities came along infrequently and were chiefly of importance to Burckhardt for the publicity they brought him and the interest in stamp collecting that they stimulated.

Patricia Spearman stood nearby and watched with great interest the conversation between her father and the eminent dealer. She had grown up on stories about some of Burck-hardt's coups in the stamp-collecting world which her father related at mealtime. Burckhardt chose to live in Cambridge, not far in fact from the Spearman home. But up to now Patricia had never laid eyes on the gentleman. What she saw was nothing like what she had imagined. She had imagined a slim, rather dashing figure—a cross between David Niven and William Powell—a person who with the slightest levi-tation of his little finger could outbid the crowned heads of Europe. What she saw was an elderly man whose dark vest strained against the sizable paunch encased within it. Spidery arms that gestured expansively contrasted with the portly girth of his trunk which itself was set upon two spindly legs. On his feet he wore high-top orthopedic shoes. The distin-guishing feature of his round face was the protruding brow that overhung the top of his eyeglasses. His complexion was pale, heightened by the darkness of the fabrics that he wore, and his large mouth, shaped like a half-moon, smiled with amusement at his customers.

"I want to offer my congratulations to you for acquiring the British Guiana one-cent. I drove over one afternoon just to see it when it was on display," Henry Spearman said to the shop's owner.

"I was most fortunate," Burckhardt responded. "A broker from Holland, representing a collector from Singapore, I am told, had instructions to go to three quarters of a million dollars, being quite confident this would be more than adequate. My instructions were to go to eight hundred thousand. But no more. So it was a close call. At those prices, one hates to lose out by a few thousand. For me, that means no commission at all." Burckhardt then smiled and looked at Spearman directly. "It must puzzle you as an economist that such a trifling piece of paper could sell for so much. Or am I wrong, Professor?"

"Well it certainly is true that for its size and weight it is the most valuable object on earth. But I am not at all surprised at its price. There's no relationship at all between the size of an object and its value in the marketplace."

Burckhardt gave Spearman his half-moon smile. "But I must tell you, Dr. Spearman, it seems odd even to me that when that stamp was issued at Demerara, the local postmaster simply printed some provisional stamps during an emergency when he ran out of stamps from London. He used ordinary type and a small ship design he got from a local newspaper. Then he added a Latin quote and to protect from forgery the assistant postmaster put his initials on the stamp. For that little bit of effort to fetch such a large amount of money is quite astonishing, you must agree."

"It would only surprise someone who mistakenly believes that the effort expended to produce something determines its value. Many economists once believed that, and the followers of Karl Marx believe it today. But in fact the market price of your British Guiana stamp is itself a contradiction to that belief."

"Tell me why, Professor. It might alleviate the shock for some of my customers when I tell them what little patches of paper now cost."

"I can well imagine their shock because people are so accustomed to thinking of price as approximating the cost of production, as it usually does under conditions of free competition. But in the case of the stamps that interest your customers, where the supply is fixed, the price placed on them is strictly a matter of subjective evaluation. How much that stamp is worth is the maximum amount that anyone is willing to pay to get it. And that amount is determined by how much gratification the buyer gets from possessing it."

"But some of my customers have bought stamps strictly as an investment, a hedge against inflation, and get no joy whatever from the stamp's possession—contrary to the way a true philatelist would."

"The joy they get from the stamp's possession comes from knowing that they have a secure investment in a time of inflation. It makes no difference whether one customer's gratification comes from the stamp's uniqueness or another's gratification comes from the stamp's ability to protect against rising prices. Subjective evaluations still determine willingness to pay."

"Interesting observation. I shall try it out on my next recalcitrant customer."

"Mr. Burckhardt, Mr. Burckhardt. Excuse me."

"Yes, my dear?" The demeanor of Christolph Burckhardt went through a sudden change, taking on an avuncular aspect. To Spearman, the woman who approached Burckhardt looked as young as some of his undergraduates. Her green cashmere sweater coordinated pleasantly with her tartan plaid skirt and Bass loafers. She was the type of woman who would be pictured in a Bermuda travel ad found in one of those airlines' magazines placed in the seatpocket, shown wearing topsiders and a sports ensemble by Ralph Lauren.

"I'm sorry to interrupt you. But do you remember that you were to call Mrs. Ridpath with a quotation on the Montevideo 'Suns' at two this afternoon? You know how she is about punctuality."

"That matter has already been addressed, Melissa. I spoke with Mrs. Ridpath this morning. Professor Spearman, I would like you to meet a very special member of my staff. This is Melissa Shannon." Burckhardt had taken her hand in his as he spoke.

"Are you Professor Spearman, the economist?" the perky young lady asked. Her raised eyebrows showed her anticipation.

"Yes," Henry Spearman replied. "And this is my daughter Patricia."

Melissa Shannon's glance went to Patricia Spearman, then returned to Patricia's father. "Oh, I've heard so much about you. Dennis Gossen is one of my closest friends. And is he a fan of yours!" Melissa's face was enthusiastic.

"Gossen? A friend of yours? I've never heard you mention his name, Melissa." Burckhardt was staring at her. "Does he live here in Boston? Where do you know him from?" The series of questions by Burckhardt surprised Henry Spearman.

"Dennis Gossen is my junior colleague. And a very talented

young economist," Spearman replied, responding more to Burckhardt than to Melissa Shannon.

"I see. A talented young man. Why haven't I heard of him before, Melissa?"

"I thought I had mentioned him to you."

"No, I am certain that I've not heard his name until now."

"Well in that case, you really must meet him. Though I'm certain Dennis has no interest in philately."

"I wouldn't hold that against him, Melissa. Not at all. You must bring him around sometime. Any friend of yours I welcome as a friend of mine."

The conversation ended with the arrival of the clerk with the stamp. "Here's your Black Jack, sir. I've already boxed it for you. Will that be a charge?"

"You may charge it to the account of Professor Henry Spearman, Phillip," Burckhardt offered.

"That will be fine. Incidentally," said Spearman as he placed the small package into his coatpocket, a glint of mischief in his eye, "if your clerk has made a slight error and Dean Clegg upon opening his gift finds a black-on-magenta octagon-shaped stamp bearing a picture of a ship, surface slightly rubbed, postmarked Demerara, and initialed E.D.W., Clegg's thank you note to me, however eloquent, would be totally inadequate."

8
Saturday, December 22

Morrison Bell looked up at the sky. To the north he saw the dark cumulonimbus clouds of a front moving in. To the south the sky was still lapis lazuli. He watched the clouds attentively for several moments. The weather station that morning in Boston had predicted more snow. And his own observation squared with that forecast. Many New Englanders paid close heed to the weather because it could affect their transportation habits to and fro. Bell was not part of that group because his house was close to the university and, regardless of weather conditions, he walked to the university. His sensitivity to the weather had another source. He was part of that determined minority of New Englanders, birdwatchers and feeders, for whom the weather was all-important. The more severe the winter, the greater would be their endeavors on behalf of these creatures. Like many of his friends in the Sierra Club, Morrison Bell would in a season dispense several bushels of seed until the arrival of spring when the birds could more readily fend for themselves.

Protected from the chill in the morning air by his heavy wool shirt, Bell made his way from the garage into his backyard. He carried in his right hand a bucket containing mixed seeds; on top of the seeds sat a glob of pale yellow suet. Bell knew the birds needed the seed for energy, and eating suet kept them warm. In his left hand he held a hammer and a scoop. The scoop he would use to funnel the seed into the tops of his three cylindrical feeders. The hammer would then be used to nail the suet to a low limb of the gray maple tree, barren of all its leaves, that sat directly behind the three feeders. These feeders were arranged so as to give the Harvard mathematician a clear view of his guests through the expanse of glass that formed the back wall of the Bells' master bedroom.

Bell's breath glistened against the Lucite tubes as he reached up to pour the food supply into the feeders. Then he checked the anti-squirrel devices on each one. For several winters he had been outsmarted by squirrels that consumed the seed intended for the birds—and the process of shooing them away interrupted his birdwatching. This winter Bell had outfoxed the squirrels. He had taken a thin metal pipe, slightly larger in inside diameter than the heavy pipe on which a feeder was supported but only half as long. This he used as a sleeve over the main support pipe. The sleeve was held at the top by a cable that went over a small pulley at the base of the food cylinder. The cable was rigged to go back down inside the main support pipe. At the end of this cable was a counterweight, only slightly heavier than the sleeve but small enough to move up and down freely in the support pipe. Thus the sleeve normally covered the top half of the support pipe, held there by the pressure of the weight.

Bell had watched with both amusement and glee as squirrels, who had figured out how to climb poles with all manner of obstacles built around them, would make their ascent halfway up the support pole. By then they were confident of their ultimate destination. But upon grasping the sleeve, their own weight would pull this sliding pipe, with them holding on, back to the ground. When they released their hold, the sleeve rose to its original place. From experience, Bell presumed that the squirrels would eventually best him at this game. But for now he had won this skirmish between man and beast.

Morrison Bell had a busy day ahead of him, but he reserved a portion of his weekend mornings for birdwatching. When at home, his hobby was pursued with little inconvenience; Bell, a resourceful man, had positioned his bed to face sliding glass windows that looked out at the yard. Since birds feed in a sporadic manner, he would prop himself up in the bed, his current work materials at his side. Within easy reach were a pair of binoculars for use when a favorite species swooped down to dine. A journal was kept on his nightstand where he recorded observations of unusual varieties.

In the spring, when feeding was unnecessary, Bell was part of that serious group of birders who frequented the nearby Mount Auburn Cemetery. Located on the flyway, it was a birder's utopia, particularly in the first half of May when many species were migrating. So passionate was Bell for this avocation that he had a key to the cemetery's gate to permit him entry early in the morning before it opened.

On this day Bell's top priority was to get through the remaining folders of the candidates for promotion. Just before his backyard visit to the bird feeders, he had completed the material pertinent to the natural sciences. Now he turned to his review of social science dossiers.

Already the feeders had attracted a congregation of blue jays and sparrows, but nothing that would warrant his particular attention. With luck there eventually might be a slate-colored junco or even a white-winged crossbill. But nothing as yet seemed worth a second look. And so Bell resigned himself to the chore of reading another file.

The first one at hand was the candidate being fielded by

the Economics department. As he looked through the titles of the reprints, Bell was relieved when he noticed that one of the publications dealt with a subject that interested him greatly, environmental pollution. It also pleased him to see that the method of exposition was in his favorite language, mathematics. The piece was a brief one, what in academic literature was called a note. The title was, "Bidding for Pollution Rights," written by a stranger to Bell, a young man named Dennis Gossen. The argument was quickly revealed, and although stated in symbolic form, could be compressed into a few words: to achieve any standard of air pollution determined to be desirable by a regulatory agency, business firms should be permitted to bid for a license to pollute. In this way, Gossen claimed to demonstrate, the standard of air purity could be attained at the least total cost to society.

"License to pollute" reminds me of James Bond's license to kill, Bell thought to himself. The very term was offensive to him. Why not sell licenses to rob and rape as well? Bell instead wanted legislation that once and for all would eliminate pollution from the air. And he had many friends who agreed. His concern was not only for his own well-being, nor was it limited to his affection for wildlife. Morrison Bell and his wife both shared a common dread that air pollution in New England, especially sulphur dioxide emissions from factories in their area and acid rain from the Midwest, would harm the health and longevity of their two daughters. Bell had at one time seriously considered a teaching post in the Southwest, in order to take his family to what he thought was a safer locale. Instead he had decided to remain and, through his Sierra Club associations, work to improve the environment. His concerned colleagues in the Mathematics department agreed wholeheartedly that pollution was a major problem.

He could not imagine one of them being persuaded that the manufacturing plants of New England should have access to licenses to pollute.

Bell put the reprint down and gazed out the window. At that moment no birds were present at any of the three feeders. No squirrels were trying to pilfer some seed. The yard was empty of wildlife. To Bell, such scenes were a foreshadowing of what the future would be like if the environment were not cleansed. And to Bell, an article like the one by Gossen only played, however subtly, into the hands of those special interests that did not want cleaner air and water.

Bell was no political radical. He did not consider himself to be anti-business. Indeed in outward appearance he and his family were a stereotype of upper-middle-class America. What bothered Bell about Gossen was that the economist seemed to accept pollution as inevitable. He only wanted to produce it at the least cost. How absurd! Where in all his equations does he make room for more abundant birds and beasts and fish and vegetation? And where is the equation for healthy lungs and longer life spans? What a wonderful example, Bell thought, of Oscar Wilde's economical description of a cynic: someone who knows the price of everything and the value of nothing.

His thoughts were interrupted by a flurry of activity at one of the feeders. He glanced outside and saw a white-throated sparrow. The bird was perched alone on a feeder dowel, proudly sporting its black, white, and yellow striped cap. A sunflower seed in its beak was devoured quickly, and with a staccato-like motion of its head, it snatched another. Bell cautiously reached for his binoculars for a close-up view of a bird he had not seen all winter. The field glasses in place, he remained motionless on the bed so as not to startle the creature. All thoughts of promotion committee matters vanished.

The ring of his bedside phone forced his attention elsewhere. To his amazement, the caller was none other than Dennis Gossen who urgently wanted to see him.

Shiny brass pots and pans hung from an oval rack positioned above the butcher block table. The table was centered in the spacious kitchen that was Foster Barrett's pride and joy. Two skylights on the south edge of the ceiling allowed the bright light of the winter sun into the room. Delft tiles lined the walls above the back edges of the countertops, giving the room a decorative elegance that softened the functionalism of the kitchen's technology. Resting on the butcher block table were half a fresh pineapple and several stalks of celery. Foster Barrett selected a sharp knife and began to slice the celery into diagonal paper-thin strips. The Harvard classicist was preparing his Saturday repast.

Saturdays were special to him. He always reserved the mornings to experiment on a new dish that would serve as his lunch and, if it passed his critical scrutiny, might grace the table at one of his celebrated brunches. Barrett's preparation for the meeting of the promotion and tenure committee had interrupted his routine this Saturday—there was still much material to be studied before January 8th—and so his culinary hobby had been cut short. He was experimenting with a Crabmeat Louie whose ingredients did not take undue time in their assembly. There was no actual cooking, so Barrett could work while the celery and pineapple were steeping in the Grand Marnier.

Foster Barrett was surprised to find himself on the P and T committee, for he knew he was not well liked among elements of the Harvard faculty. It was not his scholarship that caused disapproval. Far from it, for Barrett had set high standards there. But he also had standards about family roots, "breeding," as he might put it privately, and he wished these standards were applied to the faculty. Instead he found himself increasingly among a community of scholars from a variety of ethnic and national and economic backgrounds, with the institution itself operated by administrators who seemed to care less and less about the family pedigree of applicants to the university. At one time, earlier in his career, he would be asked occasionally by the admissions office for details about the family background and connections of a potential student. And Barrett was led to believe such things mattered, just as SAT scores and grade point averages counted. Now it was rare for his knowledge about New England's blue bloods to be sought out. Moreover, he perceived that the inner rings at Harvard were less likely to be occupied by what he classified as the right people.

To Foster Barrett, this was unfortunate. He did not like to think of his alma mater, and now his employer, as a melting pot. He preferred it to train the best and the brightest, not just the brightest, and if a choice between the two had to be made on occasion, sacrificing native intelligence for better genealogy would yield a graduate who fit better Barrett's ideal of the Harvard alum.

Before entering the kitchen, Barrett had been reviewing the information gathered by the Dean's office on the candidates. A handful he had encountered at the faculty club. Among the younger scholars he found few who appreciated the social traditions that had once graced faculty relations. Most were ignorant of the heritage of the institution and, Barrett suspected, if informed, they would not care. As he reviewed their work in the files, he saw scant appreciation of what he called "the integrative fabric of the liberal arts." These were specialists: junior faculty who sought not to know the breadth and scope of intellectual inquiry but instead tilled only the tiniest corners of their fields. He picked up at random the folders of a young astronomer and a mathematician. Were he to ask them about the Greeks, he suspected their thoughts would turn first to sororities and fraternities.

Barrett returned the folders to the dining room table where he had been working and walked to the kitchen. He took a half pound of fresh lump crabmeat from its container and prepared to combine it with the sauce that he had made an hour earlier, taking care not to break the lumps as they were turned into the sauce. As he did this, his eye caught the price on the package. This was not an inexpensive lunch, he thought to himself.

Here was another thing that galled Barrett. His social obligations resulted in considerable expense. A weekend brunch could easily provoke a five-hundred-dollar outlay for food and drink. And his summer home on the Cape had become a considerable financial drain. The economic fortunes of his family, once substantial, had fared poorly with the demise of New England's shoe industry. Now he was largely dependent upon his professional salary. And he knew this was less than many of his colleagues in other departments received.

Salary scales in universities seemed to him wholly irrational and arbitrary. Why should a physicist or an economist fresh out of graduate school receive higher pay than an established scholar in the humanities? He had heard of such things happening at Harvard, and he considered it symptomatic of the warped values that had come to dominate the institution. Even more outrageous were the salaries being paid at Har-

vard's Graduate School of Business. Rumor had it that a newly
hired assistant professor of accounting, of all things, made
more than many tenured members of such departments as
English, foreign languages, history, and his own.

Barrett spooned the concoction he had prepared over sliced
tomatoes he had arranged on his finest bone china. He took
the plate into the dining room and placed it at a table setting
he had prepared earlier. Opening a small bottle of chilled
Chablis, he sat down and nestled his chair up to the table,
his back to the kitchen. He unfolded his linen napkin and
placed it on his lap. Barrett looked down with satisfaction at
the Crabmeat Louie and edged a small portion onto his fork.

Not bad, he thought. A little less liqueur next time, perhaps,
and a dash more white pepper would do the trick. He took
another taste, savoring the mixture of flavors. Barrett bit into
a small cracker, looking straight ahead. A suggestion of a
frown crept upon his lips as he thought of the perpetrators
of some of the articles he had read earlier that day. Their
interests were so narrow. And their imaginations so con-
stricted. What did they know of Crabmeat Louie, when their
taste buds were paralyzed by plastic food. Barrett took a sip
of wine and allowed his nostrils to enjoy its bouquet. He
sighed as he scanned his table. "All of this cost me a good
deal of money," he then murmured. How unfair and ironic
it was that those with the most elegant tastes on a university's
faculty seemed always to receive the poorest salaries. His
friends in French Literature and in Philosophy had often made
the same observation. Sometimes it seemed as if life's worldly
goods were distributed through some perverse lottery. Take
for example that economist whose reprints he had been reading before lunch. Now there was a Philistine if ever there
was one.

Barrett had skimmed Dennis Gossen's work and had seen enough to know that Gossen, a man so concerned with the narrow pursuit of self-interest in the marketplace, would have little interest or use for a bottle of Montrachet. Yet Gossen could afford such a luxury more easily than a refined Classics scholar of the same reputation.

Barrett reflected on how far young economists such as Gossen had strayed from the original definition of economics. To the ancient Greeks, economics meant literally the proper management of a household. In that sense Foster Barrett considered himself to be more the true economist than was Gossen, the professional economist up for promotion. Gossen's idea of managing a household economically probably would involve taking his family to McDonald's, which would cost him a good deal less than Barrett had to pay for the lunch he had just consumed. A cultivated person with exquisite tastes like his own surely needed more money than a bourgeois colleague.

As he cleaned his plate of a final morsel of crabmeat, Barrett decided that in a just universe money payments would be in proportion to the refinement of tastes.

It was midnight and the aisles were clear. Sophie Ustinov always waited until this hour to shop for groceries. She would never become accustomed to the American supermarket, even though she had lived in the United States for over twenty years. She swept through the aisles, a store basket hanging from her sturdy right forearm. Her pocketbook was tucked against her side and locked there by her elbow. She did not like to grocery shop and moved briskly in order to get the onerous task over with as quickly as possible. Nightclerks who stocked the shelves at the Cambridge supermarket nearest her home were accustomed to her no-nonsense tours up and down the aisle and had given her the nickname Professor Gangway. She seemed oblivious to their existence as she hastily made her selections. Muttering to herself, Sophie Ustinov's judgments were audible to any shopper who could have kept abreast of her.

"No good, no good, no good." Her free hand moved rapidly as she turned apple after apple seriatim, giving them an expert once-over. Finally she raised her hands in a gesture of dismissal as she rejected the entire batch. "All are no good. And they call these apples Delicious. There's not a delicious one in the entire bunch. Tasteless they are; delicious they're not." Sophie Ustinov believed that Americans did not know how good an apple could be. The Russian apple was truly delicious. As a small girl, she remembered picking them off the tree in her uncle's yard. Tart but not sour; sweet but not cloying; crisp, not pithy. And cherries. In over twenty years she hadn't had a respectable cherry.

But her nostalgia for Russian fruit was not strong enough to cause her to return to the motherland. She had left for good with her parents in the confusion after the Great War. And nothing about Soviet communism attracted her. She was descended from the aristocracy, and communism was antithetical to what she believed to be a civilized society. The fact that the Communists had confiscated the land and homes and possessions of her parents and grandparents also had not endeared the Soviets to her. As a little girl, living with the stories about servants and not their services, she had dreamed of what life would have been like for her in a more aristocratic society. But those dreams had ceased when she and her parents arrived in New York. Since then she had determined that the mold for her life would be cast in America. On her arrival, she had studied American and English literature, to acquaint her with the West, and she developed an abiding passion for poetry—"instinctive for a Russian," she would say. But for a vocation she had pursued studies in the natural sciences. By dint of hard work and a flair for the experimental method, she had established her reputation as a world-class organic chemist.

Professor Ustinov, having declined the store's offerings in fruit, moved swiftly away from the produce counter, made a sharp turn to the right at the end of the aisle, and cantered past the dairy section, retrieving a container of sour cream, a carton of eggs, and a package of Muenster cheese. Another sharp turn, this time to the left, brought her past a long aisle that contained nothing but cleaning agents.

"Foolishness, look at this foolishness. All this stuff on the shelves. One good brand would be enough. An aisle could be five feet long instead of fifty." Her dark eyes scanned the rows of cartons and containers.

"Here it is: bleach." Without hesitation, she selected the lowest priced container of liquid bleach and placed it in her basket. "Don't they know bleach is bleach? Five and a quarter percent sodium hypochlorite solution. It's all the same. To pay a higher price is ridiculous," she continued to mutter to herself. "Ahh, but then there is that fellow—what was his name?—Gooseman? Gassman?—what did he say? He wrote an article. What did he call it?—the right number, no, the optimal number of brands."

Sophie Ustinov had just completed reading a number of candidates' files for her assignment on the promotion and tenure committee. As a chemist, she had been surprised by Dennis Gossen's article, which supported the view that there

is a finite range of brand proliferation that benefits the consumer. He had purported to discover the theoretically optimal
number of brands, a range that if exceeded or not met in
number would lessen consumer welfare.

Sophie Ustinov knew that many products sold under different brand names were chemically identical. Liquid bleach
was only one case in point. One of her colleagues in the
chemistry department at Harvard had consulted for a prominent manufacturer of evaporated milk. He had told her that
the evaporated milk sold under that company's name brand
was the same as the evaporated milk the firm sold to grocers
for their private labels. And yet their prices were significantly
different. And she knew that aspirin was acetylsalicylic acid.
Consequently she always bought the cheapest brand. "If Mr.
Gooseman knew some chemistry, he would have reached
some quite different conclusions," she murmured as she
shopped. "One brand is all you need."

After several more forays, with her shopping basket now
almost full to the brim, Sophie Usinov made what was always
her last stop before the checkout stand. Here her pace slowed.
Buying for Natasha, her Borzoi hound, required more deliberation. Only the best would suffice. And when it came to
dog food, Natasha's mistress judged quality by price. In addition, there was the variety to consider. Perhaps there would
be a new flavored dog food or a new toy on the market.
Natasha, after all, became bored with the same food day after
day. And she tired of, or else devoured, a toy after a week's
use.

Sophie Ustinov surveyed the array of pet foods and pet
supplies. Her scrutiny was soon rewarded. A new brand of
dog treats was being introduced called "The Growling Gour-

met." There were a number of exotic flavors already available, but one in particular caught her eye—Blini and Caviar. Selecting a box from the shelf, Sophie Ustinov made her way to the checkout stand.

9
Monday, January 7

The walk and steps of the Spearman home had been swept clean of the light afternoon snow. The porch lights at the top corners of the entrance cast soft oval hues against the front of the house, beckoning guests into the home's spacious parlor. The date was January 7th, in the early evening. The affair was a social gathering for the members of the promotion and tenure committee. Its purpose was a dual one.

Most members of the committee had welcomed the idea of a break-the-ice meeting prior to the marathon session of intense deliberations that would begin the following morning. The committee would have to work both productively and harmoniously to move through its agenda and reach decisions with the desired unanimity. But there was a second item on the social agenda, known to all but one member of the committee, the Dean. Henry Spearman had informed the others that on this occasion he planned to surprise Denton Clegg with a gift, to commemorate both his tenth year as dean of the faculty at Harvard and his sixtieth birthday. The esteem and even affection with which Clegg was regarded by virtually all of the senior Harvard faculty—a bond between faculty and administration almost as rare as the 1856 British Guiana one-cent black-on-magenta postage stamp—prompted almost every member of the committee not only to applaud the idea of surprising Clegg in a special way but to insist on contributing to the gift's purchase.

Henry Spearman had the Black Jack wrapped in a small presentation box, and he had also invited Christolph Burkhardt to join the evening's activity an hour into the party, when the gift was to be presented. To have arrived earlier, Burckhardt's presence might have reduced the element of surprise. For Denton Clegg was a serious stamp collector and a frequent customer of Burckhardt's establishment.

Pidge Spearman smilingly passed among her guests with a tray of colorful hors d'oeuvres she had prepared earlier that day. Henry saw to it the visitors were provided with liquid refreshment. "Pidge, you must let me have the recipe for this delicious canapé." Foster Barrett had followed Pidge back into the kitchen. "It's simply marvelous."

"That's easy, Foster. It's nothing but chopped cucumber, cream cheese, and parsley."

"I know, but it's all in the proportions."

"Well, I can try and reconstruct what I did. But I must warn you that as a cook, I seldom measure."

"Neither do the great chefs of Paris."

"Paris! You too have been thinking about Paris. What a pity to miss going there. You realize of course we will be so close to Gay Paree when our ship docks in Southampton." Sophie Ustinov had entered the kitchen in search of some ice cubes for her drink.

Pidge took her glass and added fresh cubes from an ice chest on the kitchen counter. "You could go to Paris on your own instead of returning with the rest of us when we fly back."

"But darlink, what will become of my Natasha when I am away for so long? She always misses me so. Even when I go away for a day or two, she sulks and won't eat anything. No, no. I will sacrifice even Paris for my Natasha." The three of them laughed. Sophie and Natasha were familiar figures on Francis Avenue. Three times a day Natasha's mistress took her for a brisk walk to the corner of the campus and back. Semester after semester, Professor Ustinov planned her class schedule around the Borzoi's matutinal, diurnal, and nocturnal habits.

Just off the parlor, a foursome huddled in cocktail party chatter. The two women were strangers and the initial conversation between them concerned reciprocal questions of how long have you been here? where do you live now? do you like the schools there? what do you do? hasn't the winter been troublesome? and the like. Calvin Weber picked at some cheese cubes he had arrayed randomly on his plate, listening to his wife's responses. He often learned about her opinions by routine answers she gave to others.

But tonight Weber was hearing nothing he had not heard or known before, so he decided to seek greener conversational pastures elsewhere. Meandering to the dining room he looked around and spotted Henry Spearman and the Bells in conversation. He hesitated before deciding to walk over since they seemed to be engaged in private palaver, to judge by their close proximity to one another. But from the corner of his eye, Spearman had noticed Weber's reluctance and beckoned to his friend. Spearman was concluding a discourse on some aspect of management.

"Just as in the business world," Spearman said, looking up at his audience, "everyone recognizes that management is a critical factor of production needed to organize other factors into a coherent team of production and distribution, so too in governmental and nonprofit organizations, the manager of the organization—whether the director of a government bureau, the chairman of an academic department, or a hospital administrator—is crucial in determining success or failure. Just between us," his voice dropped to a level a little above a whisper and his eyes made a quick scan to see who was within hearing range, "my own department is a perfect example of my point. At the present time, we happen to have a very poor manager running the organization. For ten years, when Quincy Lane was chairman, our department was a model of harmony and efficiency, not because we didn't have persons with greatly diverse interests and in some instances highly abrasive personalities. Just the opposite, in fact. But what we did have was a chairman—a manager, if you will—who knew how to bring out the best in all of us, minimizing the frictions that naturally arise whenever people of great ambition and considerable ability are forced to work as a unit."

Joan and Morrison Bell listened with interest. The discord that marked faculty relations in the Economics department was well known around the Harvard campus. But no one had ever explained its cause to them. Calvin Weber too was interested. In all the years he had known Spearman, he did not remember a single time when his friend discussed departmental politics. Weber had observed factional disputes in his own department over the years and had been amazed at the intensity of feelings that they generated. After all, the winner of any such dispute would have little to show for it: a minuscule raise, a slightly larger office, or the power to make decisions regarding graduate assistantships and visiting professorships. "So what?" Weber often reflected. To him, these stakes seemed inconsequential compared to the heat of the battle. But he listened closely to his economist friend, for Spearman typically had a fresh and unusual explanation for all sorts of commonplace phenomena.

"It's been my experience that when departments are divided,

the problem is one of differing methodologies or personalities among the senior people," Morrison Bell observed.

"No, dear, don't you remember the problems at Cornell?" Joan Bell interjected. "There the chairperson was a Machiavellian who believed in divide and conquer."

Spearman shook his head. "It isn't either, really, in our case. The department is not split. Leonard Kost, our chairman, hasn't sided with one group against the other. Nor is he Machiavellian, keeping two groups at war to strengthen his own hold on the department. It isn't even that he's got friends he rewards and enemies he punishes. Rather, with a tactic that may be unique to him, he has figured out that a department continually off balance causes power to concentrate in the chairman's office. The administration becomes more dependent upon the chairman as its channel of communication. I may not like his ends, but I must concede that he has developed highly original means to achieve them. And I am not at all sure how he does it," Spearman said with a smile of exasperation.

"Sounds to me like the tactics of Conrad's stationmaster," Weber mused.

"I'm sorry?" Spearman said.

"The stationmaster in Conrad's *Heart of Darkness*. Do you know the book?" The Bells had read the book, but it was years ago. Spearman confessed that he had never read the volume.

"Oh, that's a weakness, Henry, if you don't mind my saying so. In the story, a fellow—we know now it was Conrad himself—pilots a river steamer up the Congo, into the jungle, where he meets a stationmaster who controls his colonial operation, manages it as you would say, but he manages it through uneasiness. People under him didn't like him but they didn't fear him either. They had no respect for him. He didn't organize or innovate or plan. Nothing of the sort. He had nothing to distinguish himself as manager—for good or for ill. But he kept his position, year after year, because of the uneasiness he inspired. Reminds me of your chairman, the way you describe the fellow."

"I think that's it. That sounds like Kost. He has everyone uneasy," Spearman exclaimed. "How did they finally get rid of the fellow?"

"Sad to say, they didn't—so far as we know. He had an invincible constitution. His behavior remained unsocial. He simply outlived everybody."

"That's an ominous ending," Spearman smiled. "Fortunately in our own case, the chairman's term is not for life. In the meantime I must learn to live with the problem of an unsocial Kost."

Across the parlor, at the center of the house, stood the focal point of the evening, Denton Clegg. His deep booming voice was complemented by a distinguished appearance. This evening, as was common at his office, he was attired in a navy blazer and gray trousers, the latter matching the gray hair that set off his angular face. A man who let his accomplishments speak for themselves, Clegg was known to brag only that he could still fit into the uniform he wore during his time in the Navy. The Dean had positioned himself at an archway between the dining room and the parlor so as to survey the scene of the party and to permit himself ease of access to any guest. He knew that as dean of the faculty, many of the things he could not do on campus through formal channels of communication could be accomplished through a suggestion made, a comment or opinion offered, or a remark strategically placed at an event such as this one. He also realized that the promotion and tenure committee meeting tomorrow would involve much pressure, as candidates vied for the limited number of tenured slots available.

"Good evening, Denton. And congratulations too." Valerie Danzig, wearing a beige caftan, approached Clegg from the parlor. "I don't know which milestone is the more notable, sixty years of human existence or ten years of deaning existence. But I'm happy for you on both occasions."

"Thank you, Valerie. Thank you very much. I'm not sure I deserve any applause on either score. My sixty years of good health, I'm told, is purely a matter of genetics, over which I have no control. Although I do look both ways before crossing the street. The ten good years I've had as dean I owe largely to the faculty over whom I have even less control." Valerie Danzig smiled at Clegg's quip as he paused. "But I accept your congratulations, if you'll accept my thanks for your willingness to help out with the difficult job we have ahead of us tomorrow. I know it is a terrible way to spend vacation time. I must ask you to keep this confidential. But the Board of Overseers has made it quite clear that there can be no more than five young people promoted this year in Arts and Sciences. I trust I can count on you to have high standards tomorrow." Clegg sipped from the drink he had been holding.

"Yes, you can, Denton. I finished reading the files just this afternoon. I was determined not be up tonight after this lovely occasion."

"Very wise. Save your strength for the hard work. How about a refill on your drink?"

"I think I could use a refresher." Taking her arm, the Dean directed her toward the bar that had been set up in the dining room.

Oliver Wu watched the proceedings while standing in one

corner of the parlor. He was not a gregarious man and no longer cared much for social gatherings. He would much prefer to be at his library carrel. Still, some parties were professionally obligatory, and this one honoring the Dean he placed in that category. The Dean, he thought—an able scholar, everybody knew that, and not a bad fellow. But unlike most of his colleagues, Wu was able to hold his enthusiasm for Denton Clegg under restraint. Not that he had anything personal against Clegg. Their relationship had been distant but cordial. But Wu was only human. Denton Clegg held the post to which Oliver Wu had once aspired and nearly had attained when Clegg received the nod. Since then his disappointment had been well disguised by the flurry of scholarly output that had flowed forth without interruption over the past decade. In particular his analysis of numbers-running, which detailed the inner workings of this illegal industry, and his sociological theory of its Mafia control had gained him much attention. To the casual observer, Wu seemed totally absorbed in his scholarly pursuits. Most thought he was probably relieved not to have been deflected by an administrative appointment from the research on which he seemed to thrive.

Oliver Wu, a private and lonely man, did not share his innermost thoughts with others. But when the deanship passed him by, a deep wound was inflicted in his psyche. And far from healing, it had festered unabated. He had submerged his resentment beneath a placid exterior, and the energy that was required for such prolific output was fueled by this passion. When Denton Clegg was selected as dean, Oliver Wu believed he had lost face. It was the first time in his life that such a disgrace had befallen him.

It would have been better for all concerned if Wu had never learned the cause of his not being chosen. But an acquaintance on the search committee, not wishing himself to be suspected by Wu as opposing his selection, had informed Wu of the details. The committee, in its initial screening, had favored Wu over the other candidates. Only Morrison Bell demurred. His choice was Denton Clegg. What brought the committee around to Bell's position was the mathematician's argument that Clegg was a better scholar and would bring more authority to the crucial post of academic dean. Bell won his case by preparing a brief in which he compared and contrasted the articles and books of Wu and Clegg, using an adroit combination of professorial humor, sarcasm, and pedantry. He subtly escalated Clegg's stature as a scholar at the expense of Wu's reputation. Clegg was enthroned. When Wu heard an account of these events, he felt humiliated. He could not and would not forget.

And Morrison Bell would not let him forget. Two years ago, Oliver Wu was being considered for an endowed chair on the Harvard faculty. A chaired professorship would not have increased Wu's academic salary dramatically, but the perquisites and prestige associated with it were substantial. Mainly it involved prestige: a chair was like a trademark that differentiated the scholarly product, an acknowledgment that one brought honor above the ordinary to the recipient's academic institution. Wu would have considered the chair a balm for his ego. It would have symbolized Harvard's high estimation of his scholarly stature. A committee had been formed to assess Wu's qualifications and make a recommendation to the dean.

Wu was denied the chair. Although the committee's composition was a secret, Wu was convinced that Morrison Bell had once again been his bête noire. It didn't take him long to discover that he was right. This time the information came not from a member of the academic community but from Raymond, his cabdriver.

It is amazing what people will say in the back seat of a cab, oblivious to the presence of the driver, acting as if their chauffeur were an earless automaton. Had two members of Wu's chair committee not been so careless, Wu might never have learned that his suspicions were well grounded. These passengers recounted the virtuoso performance of Morrison Bell in scotching Wu's elevation. Raymond had been angered at the way in which one of his riders laughed while the other imitated the sarcastic tones of Morrison Bell when describing the published research of Oliver Wu. It was clear that Bell had changed everyone's mind.

Wu brooded. Suddenly his hostess approached. "Professor Wu, have you met everyone here?" Pidge Spearman wanted her guests to be having a good time. "I bet you haven't met the Bells." She made a move to take Wu's arm. "Let me bring you over and introduce you to them. I know you will like them."

Wu visibly stiffened. Pidge Spearman realized she had committed some sort of gaffe. Her guest was in a state of obvious discomfort. "Are you feeling all right, Dr. Wu?"

"To be perfectly truthful, Mrs. Spearman, I do not like to be forced upon anyone. Especially Professor Bell. I think if you checked with him, you will find the feeling mutual. I have been twice weighed on his scales and found wanting. I see no reason to give him another opportunity." With this, Wu excused himself and made his way to the buffet, leaving a perplexed Pidge Spearman.

Seated on the couch in the Spearman's parlor, Foster Barrett chatted with Sophie Ustinov. "There's really very little opportunity for it in my field, you know. I mean, the text of the

Iliad is there. Scholars can translate it, study it, and debate its meaning. But nobody would dream of concocting a new *Iliad*. At least I don't think they could. I believe there are ways of dating manuscripts, but that's beyond my ken."

"Well, there are ways of replicating scientific research in my field," Ustinov replied, "but it can be so time-consuming. You heard of the scandal in chemistry here. A brilliant undergraduate falsified the experiments being done for my colleague. Now it's all out in the open, months later, and his career is in shambles. People say he should have rechecked the student's work. But I say to them, how can you do that? Redo the hundreds of hours of experiments yourself? Why would you ever have lab assistants? Or graduate students? Or even post-docs? And what about the cost? People sa͟ science costs so much these days. Do they know what it would cost if we tried to verify everybody's research? Millions! Billions!" Sophie Ustinov tugged on a roast beef sandwich as if it might contain a solution to her exasperation.

Barrett looked at Ustinov in a puzzled way. He took a swallow of sherry and placed the glass on the table beside him. "But why falsify data anyway? Am I missing something about science? If you want to learn how one chemical reacts with another, and it goes one way, why on earth purport that it goes another way? I mean, isn't the key just to learn which way?

Sophie Ustinov placed the remains of her sandwich on her plate. A hint of a smile crossed her lips. "My dear Foster, what a beautiful view of science you have. You should be the scientist, darlink. Of course, in my field we want to test hypotheses. But most of the time—yes, I would say most of the time—there is a particular way we want the facts to go, as you put it. If the truth be known, we usually want our hypothesis to be accepted or confirmed. We care, one way or the other. It means fame—not like a big movie star or politician, mind you. You know that. But rather the best kind of applause a scholar can have—the applause of your own kind. Now why don't we applaud the poor *durak* who finds that his pet hypothesis is junk? I don't know. Maybe we should."

Foster Barrett, who ran in circles that did not often place him in the company of research scientists, did not know what to make of his colleague's remarks. Slowly, he applied a generous allotment of pâté to a cracker, smoothing it across the top the way a mason would shape mortar before positioning the next layer of brick. The two sat silently for a moment, partaking of the repast. "But Sophie, given what you say, why would a student or lab assistant falsify research? I can see why a professor might falsify results. But what's in it for a student researcher?"

"Foster, in your field you do not work in labs. You don't have the physical contact, hour after hour, day after day, with a co-worker. Do you know the bond that can develop on such a team? They have planned an entire laboratory around one experiment that will take thousands of hours. And for what purpose? If the student or lab assistant knows that purpose, can you imagine the temptations to read the data, as you put it, 'that way'? Especially if the student's career is hitched to that scientist's coattails. The pressures, Foster, are very, very great. And it's not really very hard to do. As an old teacher of mine used to say, 'if you torture the data enough, it will confess.'"

At approximately 8:30 Pidge Spearman heard the gentle rap of the knocker on her front door. She had been anticipating the arrival of Christolph Burckhardt at this time. She excused herself from her conversation with Jessica Clegg and made her way to the front door, which was pushed open before she reached it. Christolph Burckhardt was accompanying a young lady through the portal.

"Ah, Mrs. Spearman," he exclaimed when he saw Pidge coming toward him, "I thought perhaps you could not hear the knock, so I was bold enough to let myself in. I believe you do not know my friend, Melissa Shannon."

Although Pidge Spearman was not expecting a consort for Mr. Burckhardt, she moved quickly to make the young lady feel welcome. "I'm delighted to have you. Please come in and meet everyone."

"She's already met your husband when he visited my shop recently. But I am sure there will be many new faces for her to meet." Burckhardt laid their wraps and gloves across the open arms of their hostess.

"Go on into the living room and introduce yourselves. I'll join you in a moment."

Christolph Burckhardt took the arm of his companion and escorted her into the parlor where they were spotted by Henry Spearman. "Hello, Christolph, it was good of you to come. And you too, Miss ahh . . ."

"Melissa Shannon," the young woman said helpfully.

"You two have met, I believe," Burckhardt remarked.

"Yes, I do remember you. I'm glad you could come."

"Perhaps this is the occasion at which I could meet this Dennis Gossen I've heard so much about," Burckhardt then said to his host.

"I'm afraid this is the last place you could expect to find Dennis Gossen tonight. He's a candidate for promotion tomorrow. And my faculty guests are all members of the promotion committee. If Dennis Gossen were here, none of the rest of us could be."

"I'm certain Melissa would be willing to write a letter of recommendation if that would help the young man's prospects. Isn't that right, Melissa?"

Melissa thought she detected a slight sharpness in Burckhardt's voice. She pretended to ignore it, but appeared embarrassed. If Spearman noticed the edge in Burckhardt's voice, he seemed to pay it no mind as he led them over to the buffet table where Pidge had placed a fresh platter of deviled eggs, sliced roast beef, biscuits, and various relishes. "Help yourself, please," he said before he took their orders for drinks. "And take your time. I think we can make the presentation in about thirty minutes." Spearman ambled off.

"Christolph, I wish you wouldn't allow yourself to be so concerned about Dennis," Melissa whispered as she placed her hand softly on his arm. "He's a very special person, as you'll see when you meet him. Besides, no matter what happens between Dennis and me, I told you I want us to be friends. You know I appreciate your concern. I really do. I couldn't ask for someone to care more about my future happiness."

"Hallo, I don't think we've met. You must be the man with the stamp. I'm Sophie Ustinov." Burckhardt and Melissa hesitated, then turned from their private conversation to meet the gregarious chemist. Valerie Danzig was in Professor Ustinov's tow, and after introductions were made all around, Henry Spearman joined the foursome with drinks for the two newcomers to the party.

Noting that Clegg was still beyond earshot, and temporarily

out of view of their group, Sophie Ustinov asked Burckhardt about the stamp. "Oh, I'm afraid you will have to wait on that, Professor. What's in the box is a surprise to everyone but Professor Spearman and myself—and of course, Melissa knows too. Although I should tell you our host this evening has hopes that my clerk erroneously placed one of the world's truly rare stamps in this little box by mistake. Now wouldn't that surprise your dean?"

"Oh, but you know what is in the box, Miss Shannon. And how is that?" Sophie Ustinov inquired. Melissa Shannon seemed distracted and at first did not hear the question. "Are you in the stamp business with Mr. Burckhardt?"

"Oh no. I'm a graduate student, and I work at Burckhardt's part-time."

"I see, and are your studies here at Harvard?"

"No, they're at Boston University." Melissa paused. "But I'm engaged to be married to a Harvard professor."

Burckhardt look astound. "Oh, that's lovely, darlink, and who is this fortunate young gentleman?" Ustinov asked.

"Oh, I suppose I shouldn't say—at least to you all, because you know him, I guess. It's Dennis Gossen." Valerie Danzig's eyes narrowed as she scrutinized the young woman more closely. "Oh yes, we know him," Danzig said. "Some of us better than others, but we all know him. But we mustn't talk about him this evening, under the circumstances. There's time for that tomorrow."

"Christolph! What are you doing here?" Denton Clegg had just entered the parlor and was clearly surprised to see the familiar figure of his stamp dealer and neighbor. "And I see you have Miss Shannon with you too. I always strive for breadth on the promotion and tenure committee. But it hadn't occurred to me until now what a splendid idea it would be to add two professional philatelists to the group. But are you all right, Christolph? You look pale."

"I'll be fine in a moment. Just a little dizzy spell, that's all. Perhaps if I sit in this chair for a moment. . . "

"Can I get you anything?" Pidge Spearman solicitously inquired.

"No, no. Please. I'll be fine now, thank you."

"Are you sure you're all right?" Melissa asked. "Shall I take you home?" She placed her hand on his arm, but he drew it away. "I said I was fine." The tone of his voice was cold. He rose abruptly from the chair. "As I said, I am fine." He spoke more swiftly than his normal cadence.

After the half hour had passed, Henry Spearman announced, "let us get on with the presentation." The crowd gathered in the parlor where a surprised and much moved Denton Clegg heard himself extolled in a toast offered by Henry Spearman. The presentation of the gift was preceded by a learned disquisition by Burckhardt on the stamp's pedigree. Then Jessica kissed her husband on the cheek and the group sang happy birthday, Sophie Ustinov's voice rising slightly above those of the others.

To a relieved Pidge Spearman, the evening was almost a complete success. If it weren't for the matter of Oliver Wu's curious behavior, she would have considered the whole evening to have gone without incident.

10
Tuesday, January 8

"Why so quiet? You've hardly said a word since we got here."
Melissa Shannon searched the face of her fiancé for a clue.
Dennis Gossen firmly set down his coffee mug on the table,
so firmly in fact that a splatter of the steaming dark liquid
leapt onto the marble top. The coffee shop where they were
meeting was almost deserted that mid-afternoon.

"I shouldn't think I would have to explain to you why I'm
in such a mood today. You know that my whole career de-
pends upon a decision being made, possibly at this moment,
by eight people who could care less about the consequences
of their decision as far as my life is concerned. If they had to
bear some of the costs of turning a candidate down for promotion, they might make decisions different from the ones
they probably will reach."

A waitress unobtrusively lifted Gossen's mug and began
to wipe the table with a cloth. "Care for a refill?" the young
lady inquired. "Sure, that'll be fine," Gossen replied without
looking up. The waitress disappeared with his cup and returned seconds later with a fresh cup.

Melissa was not satisfied with her companion's explanation.
She had come to know his moods over the past few months.
This was definitely not an "I'm worried about my career"
mood, which usually meant a rather garrulous and flippant
attitude, full of sarcasm, with jokes about impending doom.
When in that state of mind, Dennis was not quiet but rather

more talkative than usual. This attitude was more of a "there's something bugging me about you and I haven't told you what it is yet" mood. That's when he became pensive and tightly controlled. "I know how much rides on your promotion, but I also know you well enough to know that's not the main thing that's troubling you today. It's me, isn't it? Something I've done. Why don't you tell me about it? We *are* engaged, Dennis, and if there's something wrong I have a right to know." As she spoke, the coffee mug Dennis held was at his lips, and his eyes, which were closed as he sipped his coffee, suddenly opened. She found herself riveted by an icy gaze. Slowly he placed the cup on the table and continued to stare at her for what seemed like more moments than actually passed.

"I would think you would know what's wrong. You say we're engaged. What kind of engagement is it when your fiancée goes out with her boss?"

"Dennis, don't be ridiculous. I didn't "go out" with my boss. It wasn't exactly a date or anything like that. Christolph was presenting a stamp last night, and he asked me to come along and be his companion. I thought it was nice of him to ask me. Besides, if I were trying to hide something, would I have gone to your colleague's house with him?"

"Yes, you might, if you didn't care about my feelings."

"But I do care about your feelings, I care very much. A good deal more, it seems, than you care about mine."

"And what's that supposed to mean?"

"It means that you don't care whom you are seen with around Cambridge and how that affects me."

"If you are referring to Valerie Danzig, then you can forget it. There was never anything to that. I told you before, we met at a faculty club party. And later she invited me—I didn't ask her—to join her for dinner. We were seen at a restaurant and some people, believing we were an item, began inviting us together to things. At most, that happened twice, I think. So if you've heard anything else, it's a good example of how rumors distort things. I haven't seen her for weeks."

"Well, she's not forgotten you. That was apparent last night when I met her and your name came up."

"Perhaps I'm not as forgettable a person as you think I am." Gossen paused. "So she remembers me. So what? I'm not going to try and avoid her in order to stop an unwarranted jealousy."

Melissa smiled. "I don't expect you to. And I'm not going to stop seeing Christolph Burckhardt. He's a fine man, generous and kind, and if I can help him out in little ways, as I did last night, I've got to have the freedom to do so. I need some space too, Dennis."

Dennis Gossen returned his fiancée's smile and tried to relax. He reached across the table for her hand and held it tightly. "Let's make a deal," he said. "You forget about Valerie Danzig and I'll forget about Christolph Burckhardt. There are obvious gains from trade to be made here."

Melissa Shannon allowed her hand to be held for a few moments, but the tension that should have been dispelled did not lift. She could feel it in the stiffness of his grip. Then she looked at him. There was a tightness in the muscles of his jaw and a frown on his face. "There's something else, isn't there?"

Gossen waited a long time before responding. His lips were pursed in deliberation. Should he tell her or shouldn't he? He wasn't sure. He had thought about it more than once and had always decided against it. But now she had asked him directly. This made it different. Suddenly he blurted it out in

an excited whisper. "Melissa, I'm worried. I'm very worried."
He looked around to see that they were not overheard. "There
is something on my mind. I've been carrying this burden for
days. I know you'll hear me out even if no one else will, but
you must never repeat any of this."

"Of course, I'll hear you out, darling." Melissa felt frightened. She had never seen him so agitated.

"Melissa, I know something that could be a bombshell.
The people you met last night. One of them is a fraud. I don't
just think I know this. I'm absolutely certain. The culprit has
as much as confessed it to me, although not in so many words,
and has promised to support my promotion if I'll keep quiet."

"Dennis, that sounds like blackmail."

"It didn't start out that way. You know me. I innocently
went to the person to ask about some research. You should
have heard the response. Backpedaling, dissembling, excuses
about misplaced data—I mean it was awkward. And I wasn't
satisfied at all. That night I concluded it was fraud. So I tried
at first to play this thing straight, go through channels and
all that. I thought of going to my chairman. But you know
how Kost makes me uneasy. So then I thought of going to
Henry Spearman. I admire him, and he's on the committee.
So he was a natural. But he wouldn't hear me out. So I tried
another member of the committee. Just took the first one I
could reach. But I got stonewalled there too. Then I went to
another. Turns out they aren't supposed to talk to candidates.
I thought the world had gone insane—it was so crazy. So I
decided to play the only trump card I had. I wasn't going to
let this person stop me. I've worked too hard to have my
career go up in smoke because of some charlatan having it
in for me. I wouldn't call it blackmail. It's like gains from

trade in a way. Support my promotion and keep your reputation. I keep quiet and you help me get tenure."

Melissa Shannon looked down at the table. Suddenly she
felt cold and she shuddered slightly. This was a dangerous
game. Gains from trade did not apply here. On the contrary,
in games like this there were always losers. Her fiancé was
young and too impetuous. She wished he had the counsel of
an older and wiser man.

11
Tuesday, January 8

The late afternoon sunlight through the blinds cast striped shadows across the surface of the oval conference table. The lines of the shadows were intermittently broken by piles of papers and notebooks, some stacked perilously close to the table's edge. The table was circled with dark brown Herman Miller swivel chairs, and at the base of these chairs were still more stacks of papers and notes scattered on the carpet.

The Dean's conference room was the third in a series of three adjoining rooms that served the operations of the Dean of the Faculty at Harvard. The first was a combination reception room and office for the Dean's personal secretary, a clerk-typist, and a receptionist. The room's back wall was covered by file cabinets. The second, the smallest of the three, was Clegg's office, where he did his paperwork and met with individual faculty members or small groups. Off this room through antique French doors was a conference room, where Clegg held committee meetings and at times invited small groups for cocktails or even a meal. Two of the walls of the conference room were lined floor to ceiling with cherry veneer bookshelves, and on these the Dean kept a portion of his library in anthropology and presentation copies of books given to him by faculty authors. His much more modest collection of books relating to university administration was next door in his office.

Only Oliver Wu sat at the table, seemingly engrossed in

reviewing a manuscript and consulting something he had written on a yellow pad. He gazed intently through his thick spectacles at the material while others on the promotion and tenure committee huddled about a coffee urn and refreshment cart that had been wheeled into the conference room. The committee had been meeting for three and a half straight hours and was taking its first break. The deliberations thus far had been intense but without acrimony. There had been disagreements, but the discussions had been of a uniformly even temper. As he munched on a cookie, Dean Clegg thought to himself that the purpose of the social gathering at the Spearmans' the evening before—the stated purpose of break-ing the ice among the committee members—had been well met, at least thus far. But he also realized the real test of this was yet to come. From experience he knew that committee meetings among even the most congenial and even-tempered academicians could become feisty as the meeting's longevity increased. Fatigue could set in, and demeanors that had been congenial could turn into tempers that were short.

"I think I shall have to call time," Clegg intoned, over the group's chatter. "The longer we tarry at refreshments, the longer we will be here tonight or tomorrow. Could I ask everyone to take their places? You may take your cups back to the table." Clegg motioned for the young lady from food service to remove both herself and the refreshments from the conference room, thanking her as she left.

The procedure that Clegg followed for every promotion candidate was to have the head of that person's department appear before the committee. A chair at one end of the con-ference table was kept vacant for this purpose. At the ap-propriate time, when discussion of one candidate was concluded, Clegg's secretary would usher in the chairman of the department to which the next candidate belonged. The chairman had already written a letter summarizing the appraisals and recommendations, from inside and outside the department, of the candidate's work and future scholarly potential. At the meeting of the promotion and tenure committee this information was not to be fully restated but simply put in capsule form by the chairman. The chairman also might offer personal thoughts of his or her own, which could go beyond or even conflict with the opinions of others whose views were represented in the candidate's file. But the candidates themselves were not heard from. It is one of the peculiarities of the academic marketplace—totally different from the for-profit sector—that a decision of momentous importance in the life of an employee and of the institution is made by a committee that never interviews the candidate. In most cases the individual concerned would not be known, let alone recognized, by any member of the committee. The main purpose of the chairman's presence was to be interrogated by the committee members about the candidate. After this questioning was ended, the chairman was excused, and the committee's confidential deliberations could begin in earnest.

The next department head scheduled to present a candidate's case was Leonard Kost of the Economics department. His department was fielding only one candidate this academic year, of assistant professor rank. Clegg pushed a button beneath the edge of the table by his chair, signaling to his secretary that the committee was ready to see Kost, who was waiting his turn in the outer office.

Kost ambled through the open French door and took his place in the vacant chair, nodding and giving a half wave to the committee members as he walked over. A gray and brown wool sweater rode high on his neck, almost covering the tartan tie and plaid shirt he wore beneath it. His corduroy trousers, chukka boots, and woolen socks made Kost look more fit for a hike than a presentation. He placed a manila folder he had carried into the room before him and looked at the table, as if trying to focus on the precise center of the oval.

"Leonard, you are acquainted with our procedure," Clegg said. "If you would be so kind as to summarize the work of—who is it now?—oh yes, Mr. Dennis Gossen. Does everyone have his file?"

"Thank you, Dean Clegg. As you know, our department has not fielded a candidate for promotion for the past two years. We take very seriously our responsibility in that regard and would not allow someone to pass our department review process and come before this committee whose lack of qualifications would become obvious in the course of your deliberations and reflect badly on our department's judgment. That is why I feel no hesitation in bringing forward the name of Dennis Gossen. Mr. Gossen's accomplishments over the past five years have been, in terms of quality—which is after all what counts in a scholar—phenomenal. Really phenomenal. There is simply no one in his peer group who can match him in the field of search theory. The letters we received from the top scholars in this area speak for themselves. I assume you've all read them by now. Seldom do we get a glowing letter about an assistant professor from a Nobel laureate. But it is clear that Gossen is known to everyone of importance in his field of research. I won't go any further into the specifics of his contributions but will be happy to answer any questions you may have along those lines. Let me just add that Gossen occupies a very special niche in our department that would be difficult to fill. I would hate to have to try. I can't think of anyone anywhere who could replace him."

"Professor Kost, you've made an excellent case for your candidate. And that surprises me. I should have thought that a tenured member of our faculty would be expected to be able to reason without running round in a circle."

Kost looked at Valerie Danzig and raised his eyebrows. He waited for more explanation, but none was immediately forthcoming. Finally he said, "I guess I don't get your point."

"My point," she replied rather testily, "is that Mr. Gossen writes articles based entirely on circular reasoning."

"Professor Danzig, I doubt that. But give me an example."

"All his work is rooted in utilitarianism. Psychologists don't believe in utilitarianism anymore, I'm afraid. You just don't get anywhere explaining people's behavior by saying they do what they do because it gives them the most utility. Every hypothesis he purports to test is based on that assumption. I'm no economist, but I thought Veblen made mincemeat of that argument at the turn of the century. Don't economists read Veblen anymore?"

Leonard Kost gave a smile of self-deprecation. "Maybe it's a matter of inconspicuous consumption. But I wouldn't be at all surprised to find that younger people in our profession have never heard of Veblen. The truth is he's quite out of fashion now."

"That's too bad," Danzig responded, "because his view of human nature is a lot closer to actual human behavior than the caricature found in Gossen's models."

Kost nodded sympathetically, "I understand what you are saying and you probably are right. But I don't think you can penalize a young scholar for adopting the paradigm of his profession."

At this point, Oliver Wu interjected. "I have an objection similar to that raised by Professor Danzig. It seems to me that Mr. Gossen has an outmoded view of human nature. She says he reasons in a circle. That doesn't bother me so much as long as the circle is large enough. My real objection is, and I think Professor Danzig would support me in this, is that he has a single-minded view of how human beings behave. This rationality business has really been carried to an extreme in this man's writings. I mean to a *reductio ad absurdum*. If people really went around calculating their every move the way this man assumes they do, the fabric of our society would come unraveled." Wu's voice rose and had a tinge of shrillness. Valerie Danzig was nodding her head vigorously all the while Wu spoke.

Leonard Kost was unaccustomed to being intimidated by others. He had not expected the meeting to go this way and was unprepared for these objections to Gossen's work. He began to stammer and looked in the direction of his colleague out of a sense of embarrassment and in the hope of assistance. Throughout this interrogation Spearman had been hunched over the tabletop, fingers laced together, hands clasping the top of his bald pate, while his elbows rested on the table's surface.

Spearman's silence thus far was self-imposed. From the beginning of the discussion he had felt strong objections to the line being taken by Danzig and Wu, but he knew that protocol required that Kost make the case for the department's candidate. Spearman was unaccustomed to such restraint, believing that illogical statements always required correction. And at this point he was at the limit of his patience. Spearman's customary joviality had left him. Vigorously shaking his head from side to side he interjected, "I beg your pardon. Excuse me! Leonard, I'm very much surprised that you have allowed these misperceptions to have gone on for so long unchallenged."

"I'm sorry, Henry, I . . ."

The diminutive economist waved his hand to cut off Kost's protestations. Spearman knew that most economists seldom thought about the preconceptions of their discipline. "Those objections are totally without merit. And they mustn't pass without comment. There may be deficiencies in Dennis Gossen's analytical work. I have no doubt at all that if we looked hard enough we would find something to fault. But nothing that has been said so far can in any way be taken seriously as a criticism of his work. Most of what I've heard represents misunderstandings of what the scientific method involves."

The atmosphere in the conference room had become strained. Oliver Wu's eyes behind the thick panes were concentrated on Spearman as he looked diagonally across the table. His mustache bristled and a slight twitch became visible at the corner of his mouth. Valerie Danzig also felt uncomfortable. She knew that Spearman liked the give-and-take of oral argument. She did not. Her face hardened as she sipped a cola drink that was on the table in front of her. Spearman peered across the conference table at Oliver Wu. There was a gleaming excitement behind his eyeglasses and his face broke into a smile. He pivoted his head to survey the faces of the other committee members. Then he fixed his gaze on Sophie Ustinov who was seated across from him.

"Sophie, imagine the problems you would encounter if you had to deal with molecules of sodium that were keenly interested in whether they were joined in chemical bond to chlorine."

Sophie Ustinov shrugged her shoulders in response: "Sodium and chlorine—they're not alive. They have no ability to reason or communicate. They're not like people."

"Exactly. They are not like people," Spearman responded. "Therefore they don't object or interfere with your experiments on them." Sophie Ustinov's eyes narrowed as she contemplated the problems she would encounter with recalcitrant molecules in a laboratory test. Chemicals that argued, cajoled, lied, or tried to reason with her would make life as a chemist far less pleasant.

"Economists can't use laboratories in their research—people would argue and cajole and possibly lie if you experimented with, say, their income or their assets over time. So being barred from experimenting with real participants in a laboratory, we develop theories that are evaluated, not by their realism, but by their usefulness. 'Usefulness' of course means theories that are tolerably good predictors of outcomes or have implications that are borne out in practice. It's true that economists have theories with assumptions that are unrealistic. When Dennis Gossen assumes that people are highly rational maximizers of utility, that doesn't mean he is stating a view of human nature that he believes is realistic. He is doing what has to be done to make the subject matter of his discipline empirically manageable. Utility maximization is one of the most powerful generalizations we have. Its usefulness has been borne out over and over again. All you can ask of an economist is high logical standards and corroborating empirical evidence. But the theory will be a generalization, ignoring many of the real world's details."

To this Oliver Wu asked, "Can a theory really give good predictions if its assumptions are unrealistic?"

"That happens all the time," Spearman responded. "Physicists assume perfect vacuums. They assume frictionless planes.

We don't complain to them—hey, that's unrealistic—do we? Of course not. Economists assume utility maximization and test theories from that base."

Denton Clegg glanced at his watch impatiently. He felt it was time to take the reins of the meeting. "Perhaps there are some more questions for Professor Kost," he interjected.

"Allow me one more moment, Denton, I want to return to something Valerie said."

"Henry, we've got Dr. Rose from Biology coming along soon. We need to be mindful of our time."

"Bear with me, Denton, for two more minutes because this is important. I want to return to something that Valerie said a moment ago." The Dean knew that when his friend was in a determined and didactic mood, he could not be deflected from his goals. Clegg allowed him to proceed.

"Valerie, may I attempt to show you by way of the soft drink in your hand that you are wrong about the circular nature of economics?"

"I'd be happy to be enlightened."

"There are two things about that cola that I am sure you are familiar with since they are so commonplace. Yet they have great implications for utility theory. One is that the first drink from the bottle is more satisfying than the last. The first soft drink itself is more satisfying than the second, and certainly the tenth."

"I don't deny that," she said.

"You shouldn't be so fast not to deny it. Because it is wrong. That is, it is wrong unless I am careful to specify the time period. It may be true for the tenth Coke you consume in an hour but wouldn't be for the tenth Coke you consume this month. So if you bought a hundred bottles of pop and stored them at home, you could pace yourself so that each one gave you the same amount of satisfaction. And that explains my second point. When soft drinks are dispensed in a machine, you can reach down and get only the one you paid for. Now let me ask you this. What happens when you buy the *New York Times* from a dispensing machine? You put in your coin, and the entire stack of newspapers is exposed. One hypothesis that would explain this is that purchasers of soft drinks are less honest than purchasers of newspapers. But that doesn't seem right since they are often the same people. If I were a betting man, I'd place my money on a utility hypothesis. That is, newspapers have a very rapidly diminishing marginal utility. Once you've got one copy of today's paper, there's very little marginal utility in a second. So vendors don't have to depend upon your honesty. You'll only take one even though you could have taken a dozen for the same coin. So their vending machines are very simple mechanical objects. The soft drink seller needs a more complicated machine, one that totally blocks your ablility to get more than one container unless you pay for it. This is because a soft drink not drunk today could be enjoyed tomorrow, or even next year. So one might very well be tempted to take away all that could be carried after paying for only one of them. Now I do not know any hypothesis other than diminishing marginal utility that can explain the different technologies by which we dispense such commodities."

"In other words, Henry," Oliver Wu responded, "an implication of diminishing marginal utility is that newspapers will be marketed in a different way from candy bars and cigarettes."

"Precisely," he replied.

"I see what you are saying," Wu said. "The theory has

predictive power, as you were telling us earlier. I'm not sure I ever understood utility theory in that way before."

"And of course you can see it isn't circular. Circular theories can't predict."

"Henry," Valerie Danzig said, "could I persuade you that you are wrong about marginal utility if I showed you ten copies of yesterday's paper frozen solid in my freezer?" The laughter in the room was led by Spearman himself.

"If you have frozen newspapers I'd predict that you have a fish wrapped in each one. But if not, and if what you say is true, well I just have to remind you that we economists never said that *everyone* is rational."

Dean Clegg endeavored to bring the committee back to the business at hand. "Ladies and gentlemen, I must play the heavy and call an end to these pleasantries. Perhaps some of you have further questions for Professor Kost."

"Professor Kost, I have a question." Sophie Ustinov sat forward in her seat and swiveled to face the economist straightaway. "You told all of us earlier that Gossen would be hard to replace, that there's no substitute for him. Well, I have read his work, and I should tell you that I have my doubts. I'm no economist, mind you, but I do shop, and I keep my eyes open. All of us here do, don't we?" Ustinov asked rhetorically as she glanced round the table. "Gossen wrote about the optimal number of brands we should buy. Well . . . he should go with me to a grocery store and try and sort out what to buy. Has he ever done that, I wonder. What would be truly optimal is if there were one good brand." Each of the last three words of this sentence Ustinov said slowly and with emphasis. "Just one. I'd take it, pay my money, and leave. Now what's optimal about having more than that? You tell me."

"Well, Professor Ustinov," Kost began, "if you had only one brand, as I suspect you encountered in Russia, you would have a state-run monopoly . . ."

"No, I'm not talking about Russia. That's, what you say, a red herring. I don't want the government running the economics. That doesn't work. Believe me, Professor Kost, I know. What I mean is just one, private, United States company producing each good people want. Can you imagine the waste in advertising different brands that would be saved? Your young man ignores that."

"What you would have then is a monopoly. In economic theory we have a . . .," Kost started to reply.

"So the government regulates the monopoly," Sophie answered back before Kost had completed his sentence.

"Now Sophie, let's be fair to Dennis Gossen—*and* consumers," Henry Spearman exclaimed. "You may not care about the differences between brands of detergents or automobiles. But I suspect you appreciate differences in chemistry textbooks; and anyone who knows you would predict you'd not be pleased if there was only one brand of dog. What if that breed was the English bulldog or the Yorkshire terrier and not the Borzoi? What Dennis Gossen was trying to do in his article on the optimal number of brands was tackle one of the more difficult questions in economics. He began with the assumption that consumer preferences are diverse, as yours are from those of other people, and he posited an economy where privately run business firms appeal to these heterogeneous preferences. But like everything in life, variety has its costs, especially if there are economies of large-scale production in making one particular brand. Gossen sought to examine how a free market economy makes that trade-off."

"But Professor Spearman, whenever you have this variety, this differentiation, you have companies adverising each brand. And advertising has its costs. Let me ask you this. How much less would I have to pay for something if it weren't advertised, if there weren't the different brands that this young man"—here Ustinov held up Gossen's stack of papers—"applauds? I ask you now. How much less?"

"I'm afraid you'd pay more," Spearman responded.

"More?" Sophie was not the only one in the room who looked surprised at Spearman's answer. "If businesses didn't spend all this money advertising, I'd spend more? Gossen may believe that. But you don't, do you?"

"Oh, I most certainly do," Spearman said, his right hand lightly drumming the table for emphasis. "If you have a product selling in one state where it's not allowed to be advertised, and the same product sells in a nearby state where sellers advertise the product, and that is all that is different between the two situations, let me assure you the product will sell for less in the latter state. Advertising is a cost of doing business. Let's be clear on that. But advertising also informs us of other alternatives. It gives us more information about what's being sold in the marketplace and about the availability of competing products." Here Spearman pointed to the ceiling with his index finger, a gesture his students knew was associated with a conclusion. "So competition is increased by advertising, and the result is lower prices for customers, not higher."

"That seems counterintuitive to me, Henry," Morrison Bell interjected.

"I'm not speaking about intuition here. Nor is Gossen. Absolutely not. There's empirical evidence on the point. Sophie, let me ask you this. In Russia, if someone had saved up to

buy an appliance, like a stove or refrigerator, where the government controlled the production, how do people buy? Do
they pick out an item at random, since they are all the same?"

"Actually no, they don't. At least if they're smart. You take
trying to buy a stove. There is more than one stove factory
in Russia. They're all supposed to make the stove to the same
government specifications. But they don't. One factory, I think
it is in Leningrad, that's the only one in the country that
makes a decent stove. So people try and find out: did this
store's stoves come from the Leningrad factory? And you
hope the one you can buy is from there. But it's hard to know.
They look alike. But the one, it is better."

"That's exactly the function of a trademark or a brand in
a free market economy, Sophie. What Gossen tried to clarify
was how the branding of products gives manufacturers in-
centives to maintain high quality lest they lose the economic
value of the brand image they have developed. Take away
their right to brand the products and make people aware of
them and you take away part of their incentive to maintain
quality control." Spearman looked to Kost who was nodding
in agreement.

"But Henry," Foster Barrett interjected, "isn't what Gossen
commends ultimately a process or system that results in the
least common denominator winning—sort of like Gresham's
law, where the mediocre brands drive out the good? You may
get Gossen's contrived optimal number of brands. But they're
all so awful."

"When you say 'awful,' you're talking tastes, not economics.
If consumers have tasteless preferences, market economies
will respond with tasteless goods. But I'm afraid you are quite
mistaken in your paraphrase of Gresham's law. Bad money
does drive out good money, as Gresham taught, but there's

no scientific evidence I'm aware of that bad products drive out good products. If you know of such, I'd appreciate your acquainting me with it. A market economy produces periodicals like *National Enquirer* and *People*; these do not fit a professor's tastes. But the same economic system produces *The New Yorker* and *Harper's*; they do. So I can't agree with you that good periodicals are driven out by bad. Now as to Dennis Gossen, he takes people's tastes, however good or bad they may be, as a given. They are taken as they are. You can't condemn the man if his work doesn't elevate tastes."

Barrett had been looking at his clasped hands on the tabletop all the while Spearman spoke. Then he looked up soberly. "As King Agrippa said to Saint Paul, in a very different context mind you, 'almost thou persuadeth me.' But not quite. If a professor isn't going to elevate tastes, then I would have to ask, who is?"

The question went unanswered. "Ladies and gentlemen, I'm afraid we may be getting off track on this candidate." Dean Clegg drew everyone's attention to his end of the room. "I must serve as timekeeper and draw our discussion to a close. Leonard, unless there are any other specific questions for you—are there any . . .?" Clegg paused as he surveyed the conferrers. "If not, you may be excused as we finish deliberations on your department's candidate. On behalf of all of us, thank you for coming," Clegg added as the economist rose to leave.

"Although we've gone a bit overtime with this candidate, we'll still reserve our ten minutes for discussion and the taking of a straw vote before we call in Dr. Rose. If we need more time for discussion, that will of course be available at the end of our session. Would anyone like to lead off?"

Calvin Weber, who had been silent throughout the morning,

arrested everyone's attention with a one-word utterance. "Teaching."

"How's that?" The Dean was taken aback.

"Teaching. Can the guy teach? I've listened to the proceedings all morning and there's been nary a note about any candidate's teaching skills. Being the new kid on the block as far as P and T assignments go, perhaps the question is gauche. Well then pardon my gaucherie, but I'm asking it anyway. I find practically no information on Mr. Gossen's teaching record in his file."

Foster Barrett did not miss his opportunity. "The new kid on the block should know that every neighborhood has established customs. At Harvard we presume that anyone put up for promotion is a commendable teacher. Therefore your question need not arise at this level."

Denton Clegg's face took on an avuncular aspect. "I am afraid Foster's right in a sense, Calvin." His smile was totally ingratiating. On someone else's countenance, someone less adept at peacekeeping than Clegg, the same smile might have appeared patronizing. "Teaching prowess is presumably considered at the departmental level."

"But so is research. Why do we as a committee review a department's evaluation of a colleague's research but not its assessment of teaching? If we were candid with one another, wouldn't we have to admit that we have more confidence in judging the teaching ability of someone in another field than their research? I can't follow the statistics in Mr. Gossen's publications. The economists can do that. But given the opportunity, I suspect I could tell if he's a loser in the lecture hall."

"But research is something objective—which we can all examine. Teaching evaluations are subjective. They turn out to be popularity contests, don't they?" Morrison Bell chirped. "Besides, if teaching were to become a major consideration for promotion, we'd all have to agree to be subject to constant surveillance by our colleagues."

"It would break all custom at Harvard to have a committee audit a faculty member's classroom," Barrett added.

Calvin Weber seemed resigned to the committee's ground rules. After an exaggerated sigh he murmured, "Well, above all, let's not break any customs at Harvard."

For the next few minutes the committee did what committees of this sort do best. It exchanged views and clarified details. There was a give-and-take among its members that brought out the different perceptions held on the candidate's merits. Technical questions were put to Spearman in his capacity as representative from the candidate's field. The others would serve in this role if their department had a candidate before them. During this time, Denton Clegg made notes in silence. It was on the basis of such discussion, as well as the vote that would follow, that his own report would be based.

"Ladies and gentlemen, I must call time on our discussion. Let's take our vote at this juncture. As before, we'll proceed counterclockwise. Henry, remember this time you are ineligible to vote since Gossen is a member of your department. You have, of course, had a chance to express your views. Oliver Wu?"

"I never thought I'd find myself in the position of casting a vote in favor of a modern-day follower of Jeremy Bentham. I think if you put any ten people in the same room with Henry Spearman, they'll come out on his side—at least temporarily. So before I change my mind, I'll vote in favor of promotion."

"Sophie Ustinov?'

"With me it's like this. Economics is different from chemistry. The methods are different. What goes in one place doesn't necessarily go in another. The economists say his techniques meet their standards. Kost says the department needs him. Let's let the department have him."

"Calvin Weber."

"I vote yes on the candidate."

"OK, that's three 'yes' votes. Henry, I'll pass over you and call on Valerie Danzig."

"I'm afraid I must break Mr. Gossen's string. With all due respect to you, Henry, I don't think the man's work stands on its own merits. My vote is no."

"OK, that's three to one. Next is Morrison Bell."

"As a mathematician, I can't fault the candidate on technique. And I suppose that he is an adequate economist. But somehow or other, and I can't put my finger on it, I believe Mr. Gossen lacks moral sense. And this comes out in his work. The stuff on pollution for example. It's clever, and technically even cunning. But there's no wisdom there. No balance. No understanding of the seriousness of the problems with which he deals." Then Bell paused. "I'm not sure I should even bring this up, except I think it perhaps illustrates what I am saying about the candidate's lack of sense. He called me more than two weeks ago at my home and asked to talk about this committee. Naturally, I cut him right off. But then to my annoyance I got an envelope from him in the mail anyway. Then he called back and said he'd made a terrible mistake; that the information in the envelope was incorrect, and he'd appreciate it if I would forget it. He was profusely apologetic, asked that I destroy the letter, and not even bother to read it if I hadn't already done so. As it happens, I hadn't read it. In fact, I still have it at home. It's unopened, I can assure you—on my bedstand—where it shall remain. The point of the matter is, all this does not account for my vote. But it perhaps underscores it. I would hope this institution could do better. My vote is no."

Denton Clegg looked at Bell seriously. "Well, we can't have candidates politicking for promotions. You showed good judgment in not reading whatever he gave you." Dean Clegg scribbled on his tally sheet. "The count is three to two. Foster Barrett, that brings us around the table to you."

"I was not going to mention the matter at this committee meeting until Morrison did, although I thought it proper to share it with Dean Clegg last night at the Spearmans'. But in the interests of full disclosure, let me add that this fellow Gossen approached me as well. He started to say some rather unseemly things about this committee, at which point we had a contretemps that ended our contact. I've not seen him since. I do agree with everything said by my colleagues on my left. I don't think the man is cut out for Harvard."

"Then it's three–three and that places me in the role of tie breaker. My policy in the case of a tie, unless there are extenuating and extraordinary circumstances, is to vote no. On a matter of such importance as promotion, there should be more than a split decision needed to guarantee a person's tenure. I have no special information about this candidate that would lead me to do otherwise. Mr. Dennis Gossen is turned down for promotion."

12
Friday, January 11

The checkbook wouldn't balance. Arithmetically it was supposed to. But the figures did not jibe. Experience had taught the economist that his bank cleared checks infallibly. It was not to guard against a clerical error on the part of the Cambridge Trust that Henry Spearman monitored closely the finances of his checkbook. Rather, he sought to keep his running balance only within the bounds of his needs for ready cash, so as not to pass up higher income-earning opportunities elsewhere.

Did I slip up somewhere? Spearman wondered to himself when the arithmetic he did in his head would not square with that on the bank's computerized statement. Spearman refused to use a calculator for such tasks, because of his conviction that these devices would reduce his ability to do computations mentally, a useful skill that he believed was diminishing in the silicon chip generation. Once again he scanned the entries, until he realized that a utility bill, which was now automatically deducted by the bank, had not been recorded and taken account of in his checkbook calculations. Spearman was pleased with himself that the imbalance was the result of an oversight on his part and not due to a failure in his mathematics.

Putting his checkbook back into his pocket, he surveyed his office. It was Friday morning, the eleventh of January. In a few days the spring semester would begin, and his Friday mornings would be occupied with seeing students. His office hours fell then. But this Friday morning, between semesters, there would be no students to see. Not that scholarly journals would be studied instead. Nor would lectures be revised or research projects furthered. The frontiers of economic knowledge would not be advanced today, at least by Henry Spearman. Rather, with the time-intensive demands of the promotion and tenure committee behind him he would relax by doing some more reading in Denton Clegg's book. Denton had given him a presentation copy when it was published several months ago. But Spearman, with the unusual press of fall semester duties, had been unable to do more than barely begin the volume. Today he hoped to have a couple hours to peruse it, at least enough so that he could make some intelligent comments about it to his friend. This would leave him time in the afternoon to tackle other projects: mail that had accumulated for the past few days and the stack of pink slips, each representing a call that sought returning, sitting on his desk. The day held all the promise of being a mundane one in the life of an academician.

Henry Spearman rose from behind his tan metal desk and paced across the room to his work table where his mail lay. His secretary had opened it and placed it in piles according to a priority system he had found it necessary to develop as his prominence as an economist increased. The top priority pile contained letters from other economists of rank who sought either his counsel about economic research or his attendance at a conference. At the other end of the spectrum sat sample textbooks, often sent in triplicate copies, from publishers seeking their book's classroom adoption.

Spearman found himself tired this day, almost exhausted. The committee meetings had not gone easily, and they had taken him from his research—work he found to be invigorating rather than draining. He picked up the copy of *Mores and Manners Among the Melanesians*. Spearman knew that Clegg considered this work the capstone of his career. He had spent many years studying the inhabitants of the Santa Cruz Islands, and the results of his research would overturn established theories about the culture of islanders in the South Pacific. Spearman had left the inside flap of the dust jacket at the place of his last reading. He eased into his desk chair and began to read. This part of the study should have held more interest for Spearman than anything that he had encountered thus far. But he found it difficult to concentrate or think very deeply about what Clegg was saying. The economies of primitive peoples held fascination for some economists, but the subject matter had never attracted Spearman. The conundrums of commerce and finance in modern civilization were more than enough to keep his analytical talents busy. And he had not felt the slightest urge to delve into the warp and woof of primitive societies.

Not so with Denton Clegg. As Spearman could see from the text before him, the Dean was thoroughly enmeshed in the loom of such cultures. Even to the point of amassing data on the prices of various commodities sold in the islands. These had to be expressed in terms of a currency whose complexities Clegg had deciphered.

The primitive currency about which Spearman read and on which the entire monetary system of the Santa Cruz Islands depended was fashioned from the red feathers of a small scarlet-colored honey eater of the rain forest. These feathers were fashioned together with tree sap and fiber into a belt. Each belt had a precise value in terms of other belts, depending upon the quality of the feathers. Spearman found himself chuckling as he imagined the residents of the islands carrying sizable quantities of lengthy belts of feathers when it was time to make a major purchase. Visually, it was in his mind a remarkable contrast to a modern plastic credit card. And yet just two hundred years ago in the United States the dollar was defined as a given weight of silver and a given weight of gold. This was considered an improvement over the wampum commonly used in exchange among the Indians of North America—which consisted of strings of colored beads. Moreover, Spearman knew that if dollar bills were removed from today's economy, modern man would go back to commodities very quickly. The best evidence of this was the widespread use of cigarettes as currency in prisons and prisoner of war camps.

As he read, he thought how interested his friend Denton would be in a story related by the nineteenth-century economist, William Stanley Jevons, the father of marginal utility theory—a story that countless economists have shared with their classes concerning stages in the evolution of money. Mademoiselle Zélie, a member of the Théâtre Lyrique from Paris, was once invited to sing in the islands of French Polynesia. Her share of the gate receipts was to be a straight one third. But when the division was made, to her shock it consisted of pigs, turkeys, chickens, lemons, and cocoa beans. Back in Paris, the value of these items would have been considerable: about 4,000 francs. But she ended up feeding the fruit to the livestock, and the mademoiselle returned to France with a deeper appreciation for the virtues of paper currency.

The morning was getting on, and Spearman knew that he would soon have to get around to other chores. He decided to finish the chapter and then proceed to other matters. The material explained how price ratios were established in the islands' currency. It did not surprise the economist to learn that the value of a red feather belt is ultimately defined by some standard: in the Santa Cruz Islands, this standard was the minimum payment made to a bride's family by the groom's kin. This was the "bride price." Clegg had discovered that this standard always consisted of ten currency units and these units are graduated in value from a perfect number 1 belt to a number 10 which is the lowest valued. Clegg related in his book how easily the natives could do arithmetic in their head that at first required paper and pencil for him. The relationship in value between the gradations of belts was geometric. Each belt is worth twice as much as the one below it on the scale. Thus a suckling pig that could be bought with a single number 6 belt would require two number 7s. A container of honey that could be bought with one of the very best belts would take 512 of the very worst. Clegg had painstakingly gathered prices in terms of these belts for all of the commodities he found traded in the islands during a given month. These were listed in tables in great detail. For example, the most expensive item that Clegg listed was the canoe. The prices of canoes of comparable quality throughout the villages and islands Clegg visited averaged 950 number 9 belts. Their price ranged anywhere from 780 to 1,100 belts. A basket of yams, on the other hand, a minor item in the islanders' diet, ranged from four to five number 9 belts.

As he read, Spearman noticed a difference between his colleague's research and his own. It was considered a breakthrough in anthropology to discover and list previously unknown facts. An economist would not be as likely to list data without offering a theoretical interpretation as to the significance of the magnitudes. Nonetheless, Spearman read with pleasure Clegg's sensitivity to the importance of markets in this less developed economy. The book related the haggling that went on in various village markets and told how shoppers regularly went to different villages to ensure that they were getting the best deal for their precious red feather money. Spearman's eyes scanned again the tables of prices that Clegg had gathered and . . .

Abruptly the door to Spearman's office opened. There had been no knock or warning. "Henry, may I see you for a moment?" Leonard Kost stood in the doorway of the office, his face pale and his expression grave.

"Something terrible has happened."

"Of course, come in, Leonard," Spearman responded from beside the table, motioning to a chair near his desk. "What's wrong?"

"I just now received tragic news about Dennis Gossen. He's dead."

"Dead!" Spearman repeated the word, more as exclamation than a question. "What happened to him?"

"The Dean's office just called me, and I don't have details. But someone found him in his car early this morning. He committed suicide. Carbon monoxide poisoning. He had a hose from the tail pipe running into his car. Dennis was dead when they found him. The police discovered a short suicide note in his typewriter at his home. It was beside the letter turning him down for promotion. I had planned to call Dennis in today, to talk about his future plans, and naturally to tell him I was sorry about the committee's decision. Of course, I had no idea he'd take the decision this way. I couldn't have, could I?" Kost stared imploringly at Spearman for reassurance.

Spearman looked back at Kost and then beyond him. He found himself uncertain what emotion to adopt for these circumstances. He was sad for Gossen's family and for Gossen's fiancée, who had only recently been a guest at his home. He was troubled that the aspirations for a tenured faculty position could take on such disproportions. He regretted the loss to his profession of a young scholar with such potential. And he was angry that someone, perhaps it could have been himself, had not shown the sensitivity to prepare Gossen for the news that Spearman now learned had provoked the assistant professor to take his own life.

"Has his family been notified?" Spearman inquired.

"Yes, they've been told by the coroner's office. I understand Dennis's father is flying here today to make arrangements. I've left word with his mother that the department will help out in any way we can. My worry is that the press will make a big to-do of this. Do you think I should talk to them, Henry?"

Spearman walked to his desk chair, circled the piece of furniture once, and then plopped himself into it, facing his colleague. "I would talk only briefly with any reporters who contact you—a name, rank and serial number kind of response. They won't be interested in Dennis Gossen. They're looking for a story, probably one about how Harvard exploits its young faculty."

"You're right, Henry. I think I won't tell them anything but the essentials. The press loves a 'professor-looks-bad' kind of story." Kost prepared to leave the office. Spearman had already reached for the phone as his chairman made his retreat.

"Dean Clegg, please," Spearman intoned as he called his friend's office. "Denton? I know you've heard the tragic news about Dennis Gossen. I called to say I'm sorry for you too, my friend. I know this only adds to your burdens at this season. I won't keep you long. But I wanted to get your reactions. You and I have seen many young and able people not make the grade here. I can't recall any of them taking this extreme an action, do you? I also want to let you know that whatever you plan to do to fortify or bolster our other young scholars, I want to be available to help. I understand there can be waves associated with suicides."

"Thank you for calling, Henry," Clegg responded. "Yes, I am very concerned—most immediately about the other assistant professors who, like Gossen, have just received letters from my office with the same bad news. I've called a meeting of them and their chairpersons for this afternoon. And I've told them it is urgent they attend, in the case of the department heads, even if it means canceling travel plans. I've spoken to the counseling center and the medical school, alerting them to the situation and they are making their people available to the faculty. Frankly, I'm also concerned for our young graduate students entering the job market. What anxieties does this stir up for them? God only knows. Then there's the Board of Overseers. I've already heard from two of them wanting to know what kind of a sweatshop we run. That's the term one of them used: a sweatshop. So the President has asked me to prepare a memo on this for them. There've been faculty members who've committed suicide before, and you'd be surprised at how many over the years we've deterred through counseling. But with Gossen, there was no warning. And the action seemed so illogical. I mean, the fellow is not promoted here. Is that the end of the world? So he teaches at one of any number of good state universities. Or, there are many very solid liberal arts colleges that would snap him up. That's why his behavior seems so senseless."

When the conversation with his friend was over, Spearman returned the receiver to its cradle. The Dean's words "senseless" and "illogical" stuck in his mind. Suicide did not fit gracefully into Spearman's model of human behavior. It was his scientific conviction that individuals made marginal adjustments in their choices. They bought more of this or less of that. They moved here instead of there. They took one job instead of another. They spend an additional hour at work, sacrificing in the process a given hour of leisure. His credo since graduate school had been the frontispiece on Alfred Marshall's great *Principles* treatise, *natura non facit saltum* (nature does not make leaps). Suicide seemed to Spearman to be a leap. Conceptually he realized that an individual took his life when the discounted lifetime utility remaining to him was negative. But for a young person who had so much potential satisfaction to be enjoyed by living, such an act would be irrational.

He glanced halfheartedly at a portion of his mail and chose not even to read the names on the pink slips, much less the messages his secretary recorded beneath them. He decided that responding to mail and placing telephone calls could wait until tomorrow. He had no energy for these tasks today. Donning his hefty overcoat and cap, Spearman prepared to leave the building and make his way home.

An icy coastal breeze met him as he left the building and accompanied him as he made his way to his automobile. When he approached the parking lot proper, he was hailed by a voice from behind. "Mr. Spearman, I say, Mr. Spearman!"

Turning, Spearman saw himself being approached by Professor Foster Barrett. "Did you hear about your young colleague?"

"Yes, I just heard the news. It is very disconcerting. Economics has lost a talented scholar."

"Well, it is also upsetting in other ways. The papers have been calling me—even interrupted my breakfast this morning.

It seems that our balloting on the P and T committee is not secret after all. The names of those who voted against your man Gossen have been released to the press. Now the lords of the fourth estate call me and confront me with questions as though I *caused* the poor fellow's death by voting against him. Of course, they're too ignorant of words to distinguish between causing a death and being responsible for it. Our committee's decision in the abstract sense may have caused Mr. Gossen's death. But we're not responsible for it."

"I'm not certain how you wish me to respond," Spearman said. "I can assure you I did not—indeed I would not—inform anyone outside how you or any committee member voted on Dennis Gossen. I consider it most unfortunate that this has been leaked, as you say it has. And I certainly don't hold you responsible for Gossen's death. Not at all. You couldn't have expected a consequence like suicide. No one did. Where you and I disagree strongly concerns your vote against him, as you know. On that you were wrong, I'm convinced."

"I was *wrong* to vote against the lad? Come now, man. Surely you would agree with me now that the poor fellow was not fit for our faculty ranks. I mean, the evidence is now in, if it wasn't before. To take your life because you can't handle a little adversity? That's not the mark of a Harvard man—alum or faculty! Somewhere along the line Gossen should have been exposed to the Stoics. It may seem rather Homeric to die young. But not by suicide. Unless you do it like Socrates—nobly . . . for a cause. But your colleague Gossen takes his leave out of weakness. The ultimate in sniveling. And of course he had no regard for the fallout—the press, the rumors, the gossip, the damage to the university."

"I suspect," Spearman responded, "there is more to Gossen's death than a social blunder or a sign of weakness. At any rate I'm confident the reputation of the university will weather this tempest. There have been fouler ones before. As to the press, I suggest you tell them what you've told me: Gossen's death simply proves to your mind he's cut from the wrong cloth to be a Harvard don. That response should stop them from intruding upon your mealtime."

Spearman started his car and drove west from the university. At first, he had planned to go straight home, but he decided to make an intermediate stop at Calvin Weber's residence. After being shown into his study, Spearman told him the news. Weber said he was hearing the story for the first time. Spearman recounted how the vote on the promotion and tenure committee was no longer secret, how Dean Clegg was responding to the event, and about Barrett's reaction. From his initial response Weber had seemed to hear only the last part of Spearman's remarks.

"You know, Henry, Thackeray wrote of 'he who meanly admires a mean thing.' That's Barrett—supercilious and snobbish all at once. He believes his vote has been vindicated. He admires that in himself. But he doesn't want to be hassled about it. Did he even ask whether Gossen had a family? Or about his girl friend who was at your party? Has anyone seen whether she's being consoled?"

"I don't know," Spearman confessed. "I did want to let you know of this tragedy firsthand. I was on my way home to tell Pidge before she hears it on the news, if that hasn't already happened. She's met Gossen—in fact he was by our house one night, very distraught, about his promotion. But there's no way he could have known then he'd be turned down. In fact, given the support he had in our department, he had every right to expect the opposite."

Calvin Weber offered Spearman some hot tea, which was

declined, and then he tried to cheer his friend up by chattering about the experiences he had had purchasing clothes at Filene's on the day he had encountered Spearman unceremoniously dumped into the terrycloth bathrobes. But this effort also met with no success. Calvin Weber helped his colleague on with his topcoat as Spearman left to go home. "Remember, Henry, there was nothing you could have done. You made a strong case for Gossen at the meeting. My mother used to sing a spiritual to me about there being a balm in Gilead. Your defense of Gossen's work—your esteem for it—would have been a balm for him." Weber paused. "If only he could have known."

Spearman pointed his car south across the Cambridge suburb for the short drive from Weber's house to his own. In less than five minutes, he was home and was greeting his wife with a kiss. "Henry, I heard the news. About Dennis Gossen. I *knew* something was very wrong when he came by to see you that night." Pidge Spearman did not say it directly, but Henry knew her concern: that he had been too abrupt with his colleague the night Gossen had called upon him at home.

"And Henry, the phone's been very busy here. Let's see, Sophie Ustinov called and so did Morrison Bell and Valerie Danzig. All three of them seemed upset, especially Miss Danzig. They wondered if you knew, and I guess what your reaction was if you did. And someone called from the student newspaper—and two television stations called. One of them, I forget which now, is doing a special tonight on the faculty promotion process at Harvard. They would like to interview you. I suggested they call Leonard Kost."

"Wonderful," Spearman murmured, "a special. After a half day's research, they'll present an in-depth analysis and commentary, no doubt with specific suggestions for reform. All this cooked up instantly about an institutional process that has been hundreds of years in the making."

Spearman's voice became more audible. "Thanks, dear, for deflecting them to Leonard. I don't think I'll take any calls today—except from colleagues. If you don't mind, I'm going to my study to think. Let's go out later tonight for some Chinese food, OK? Just the two of us."

13
Saturday, January 12
Sunday, January 13
Monday, January 14

"Daddy—I can't find my violin case. Do you know where mom put it?"

"Why don't you ask your mother?"

"She's in the basement with Debbie, getting her ready for gymnastics. And Kelly's mom is waiting out front."

"Have you looked under your bed or in your closet?"

"No."

"Well, you go do that and I'll tell Mrs. Sedgwick that you'll be right out."

Saturday mornings at the Bell household started in high gear. Almost everyone had an appointment to keep. There was constant movement between the kitchen and the rest of the house as quick breakfasts were consumed in between preparations for the day's schedule. Emily, the younger daughter, had to be ready at 8:30 for the car pool to her Suzuki lesson. Her departure usually involved a last-minute emergency or two. This Saturday it was a misplaced violin case. Last week it had been her music.

Morrison Bell was relieved it was not his turn to drive the car pool this week. He knew from experience that Mrs. Sedgwick could expect similar delays along the route. His wife was in the basement laundry room, he supposed, finding a last-minute clean towel or leotard for Deborah's gymnastics class. Joan would take Debbie to gymnastics at the high school, then she in turn would go to their church for her aerobics class. This distribution of family personnel was altered at midmorning, at which time Joan would take Emily to her painting class at the Art Institute and Debbie went to a computer class; at least that was the pattern this winter. Last winter it had been a combination of Suzuki, swimming, and ballet.

"Don't kids ever go out in the yard to play anymore?" Morrison Bell found himself saying as the last of his family left the house that morning. The pattern was very different from his own remembrances of childhood. His mother would tell him and his brother to go outside and play until she called them in for lunch. In the interim, you got together with other kids in the same situation and decided what to do. It could have been marbles, or eeny-einy-over, or, if the group were larger, a game of ball, or hide and seek, or red rover, red rover. A distinguishing feature was the absence of adults in organizing the activity. In Bell's case his father went off to work every Saturday morning. He drove a dairy truck. After his dad had left, his mother's morning was fully occupied ironing clothes, cleaning the oven, defrosting the refrigerator, hanging out the laundry, canning fruits and vegetables—tasks that were done for Joan by advances in technology: wash-and-wear clothes, self-cleaning ovens, frost-free refrigerators, electric dryers, and frozen foods. Women who remained housewives in the affluent American home had now assumed the role of social director, making sure that everyone had a productive activity to engage his or her energies.

For Bell himself the activities of his family worked to his advantage. If his children played in the yard, his passion for birdwatching would be hindered if not thwarted. It was the combination of the peacefulness of the backyard and the food that Bell put out that attracted birds to the enclosed area behind the house. Bell could then watch them from the comfort of his bedroom in a way that did not disturb visitors to his uncaged aviary.

The Harvard mathematician entered the privacy of his quiet chamber. This was his favorite setting for both work and leisure. Unlike his father's occupation, where the requirements of others dictated a rigid work schedule, Bell could choose if and where he would work on a Saturday morning. The portability of mathematics journals meant that a bedroom would suffice for keeping up with the literature in his discipline. And there was no time frame for this task's completion. His material could be set aside for as long as he wished, and it would be if interesting specimens visited his feeders.

Bell placed the pillows against the headboard, slipped off his shoes, and settled onto the bed. As he deliberated about where to start in his reading, his eyes fell upon the unopened manila envelope on his bedstand. He had hoped to eradicate the memory of yesterday's news from his consciousness, but the pale-colored packet forced him to think about the tragic event he had learned of yesterday. When the unfortunate Dennis Gossen had called him exactly three weeks ago and was denied an audience, he had announced that he would be sending something in the mail. "Would you please read it?" Those were his parting words, Bell recalled. But at the time Bell considered the request beyond the pale. When, to his chagrin, the envelope arrived he placed it upon his nightstand. He thought that he might read it, but only after all deliberations of the P & T committee were over and decisions had been made. But then Gossen had called back and asked him not to read it after all. Gossen being dead, Bell felt a deep ambiguity about his course of action. On the one hand, reading it now could do no harm to anyone. On the other hand, what good could it do?

The young man had taken his own life. And Morrison Bell, in spite of himself, felt guilty. Guilty not because he had knowingly done anything that could have led to such an end. But guilty nonetheless. He had unceremoniously turned away a human being who he knew now had been in desperate straits. To make matters worse, he had voted against Gossen's promotion. True, he hadn't been the swing vote. Dean Clegg, he remembered, had cast the tie breaker. And Foster Barrett had been the last faculty member to vote in the negative. Had Barrett voted the other way, things would have been different. But this was small consolation to him. He knew that had he voted in the affirmative, there would have been no tie for the Dean to break. Still, even if he had known the eventual outcome of that fatal ballot, should he have acted any differently? Bell had chosen to vote on the merits as he saw them. He could have chosen otherwise. But so too could Gossen have chosen otherwise. He had to remind himself that nothing he did compelled that troubled young man's suicide. But regardless of what he thought, others would think differently. The media had seen to that.

In all of Bell's years on the faculty, he could never recall the secrecy of the promotion and tenure committee being breached. In the case of his first promotion he did not even know the identity of the members of the committee. That information was now available. But the secrecy of the committee's voting was sacrosanct. Bell had somehow avoided the media on Friday when they tried to interview him about his role in Gossen's suicide. And he was glad he had. He had winced when he witnessed the appearance of Barrett on the

Friday evening television news. Poor Foster. He had such a strong sense of propriety. He so much believed that what happened at Harvard was nobody's business except that of the university. And now his vote on a supposedly secret ballot had been broadcast for all the world to know. Foster Barrett, who would not be caught dead with a television set in his own living room, had now been caught live on television sets in living rooms of countless Bostonians.

But in a way it served him right. There was no excuse for Barrett to say what he said about him and Valerie Danzig. Foster had allowed the lights and cameras to ruffle him. He could have limited his answers to himself, or even evaded the questions. That's what he, Bell, would have tried to do in a similar circumstance. Barrett's underscoring the involvement of others in Gossen's act of despair was uncalled for.

Bell picked up the envelope Gossen had sent him. He realized that he did not even have a face to attach to the sender; he could not in his mind picture the young man who caused Friday's excitement and Saturday's melancholy. Bell decided finally against opening the envelope and returned it to the nightstand. On Monday, he would simply send it by the university's messenger mail to Gossen's office. Letting those responsible for Gossen's affairs decide what to do with it would be best, he thought.

Bell's eyes caught a motion among the pine cones he had spread Friday evening below one of his feeders. He pivoted his head for a better look. There could be no mistake about this one. The shape of the beak was the giveaway. Bell felt a surge of delight that dispelled all of his earlier emotions. This was to be a lucky day after all, he thought. A white-winged crossbill was right outside his window, feeding on a pine cone. A close friend from the Sierra Club had called him yesterday to let him know that crossbills were being spotted in their area this winter. A few pine cones, Bell had hoped, would vouchsafe a look. And there one was. When he and Emily had last seen a crossbill two years ago, his daughter had thought it was deformed because of the way its beak twisted over itself. Bell had taken joy in explaining to his daughter that this "deformity" was what enabled the bird to extract the seeds from pine cones. Bell took his binoculars and used them for a closer look.

The sighting of an unusual bird cheered Bell immensely. Nothing in all of nature presented such a complex physiology packaged in such striking beauty. And sightings like this one were to him vital signals that mankind was working with nature to restore the environment. He looked forward to the return of his family so he could share the news with them.

His mind had left the Gossen affair completely. Aberrations like that happened in life, he knew. But his focus today would be on that which brought him satisfaction. Bell looked at his watch. "It will be at least three hours before the kids and Joan get back," he said to himself. He glanced again at the feeding area. The crossbill was gone. Bell watched a few minutes for any other interesting activity. Seeing none, he began his academic reading.

For over an hour he read in silence, occasionally glancing up to catch sight of regular guests to the feeders. The house was very silent when the children were gone, he thought. But all that would change soon enough. He must make use of the solitude while he could. He plowed through another article. And then another. A second hour went by. Bell did not budge from his position. He found himself current in one mathematics journal and he began to skim the index to another.

His periodic glances out the window revealed much activity, but all run-of-the-mill variety. Nothing worth a second look. He went back to his reading. A sudden flurry attracted his attention. He looked up and noticed to his surprise that all of the birds were flying away. No movement could be detected either on the ground or on the feeders. The pale chunks of suet stood naked in the winter air.

He got up and walked to the window. His backyard was still. The branches of the barren trees seemed frozen in position. I wonder what frightened them, he thought. Bell stretched his arms and legs. There was a stiffness in his limbs from his immobility. He noticed that the feeders were nearly depleted. That wouldn't have startled the birds, he knew. But perhaps this would be a good time for a break. A brief foray outside would perk him up and undo the stiffness. The birds would be watching and wanting to return, and the sight of his filling the feeders would reassure their welcome. He went from the bedroom to fetch the wool shirt that served as his jacket.

Bell slid open the glass door of the bedroom and stepped into the frosty air. He trudged through the packed snow on the path that led to the side entrance of his garage. As he approached the door, he noticed that it was slightly ajar. "I've told Emily a dozen times to keep this door shut after she gets her skates," Bell sighed. Pushing open the door he stepped into the dim interior. His hand flicked on the light switch. There was no response. "Drat," he said, "the bulb must be burned out. How many times have I told the girls to turn this light off when they leave." Bell sighed again the sigh of a father over daughters whom he adored.

So often had he gathered bird feed from here that he could move automatically to the receptacles where it was stored.

So accustomed was he to this garage that he needed little light to find his way around. That is why he knew it was true—he knew it with a certainty as firm as any mathematical tautology—that he was not alone in this familiar space. He knew it before he saw anything or felt anything.

The blow fell. Soon the garage was still. In the backyard the feeders remained unfilled, the birds came and went unwatched.

Foster Barrett opened the doors of his spice cabinet and removed his garlic press, some thyme and oregano, and a bay leaf. A fresh filet of red snapper lay on the cutting board beside him. Sunday nights his club was closed, and for several years he made it his practice to dine at home alone. It was his night, as his friends knew him to say, "to savor the trinity: food, music, and a novel." Tonight's agenda would be pesche, Vivaldi, and Graham Greene.

It was 6 p.m. when he began. It would be about an hour before the meal was ready, just after dusk, he predicted. He would dine to Vivaldi's "Concerto for Two Trumpets and Orchestra in C." Then on to Graham Greene's latest novel.

Barrett socialized often. But his choice was to remain a bachelor, a confirmed one. He wanted time for solitary enjoyment of the sort he anticipated this evening. He normally did not feel alone in his house, even when he was by himself. But tonight seemed different. This evening his home seemed to lack the ambience of festivity that he enjoyed—and there was darkness that was not accounted for by the setting New England sun. Barrett strode out of the kitchen to the dining room and turned on the record player. Let the Vivaldi begin now. That ought to liven things up a bit, he thought. The Harvard classicist returned to the preparation of his meal, with the hopes that music would have charms to cure the heaviness of heart and pensiveness he felt.

Was it the events of the day with Gossen? he wondered. "Of course not! Don't be silly, Foster," he found himself muttering. "The young fool goes and kills himself; no regard for others; total disregard for his school. Colleagues with so little integrity and breeding they cannot be discreet." And then there was the cameraman who had caught him unaware in his office, filming him as a microphone was shoved toward his face accompanied by inane questions about Gossen. "What idiocy. Enough to ruin a man's evening." Barrett had determined not to watch the evening news, or the special documentary he understood was being assembled on the promotion and tenure process at his alma mater. He dreaded the prospect that some clip of the film made at his office would be shown on the news or make its way into the documentary. The whole episode seemed so pointless and in poor taste. "Of course, I've nothing to be ashamed of," he murmured. "There was no time to reflect, no time to muse."

The brilliant runs and fanfare-like music from his speakers did not enliven Barrett's mood. Nor did he find his usual joy in cooking. As he began the preparation of his evening's salad, he even began to feel cold, as though there were a dankness to his mood that made him physically chilled. He thought of calling a friend to come over, a spur-of-the-moment invitation perhaps, to join him for dinner. The snapper's size was sufficient. The salad could be easily expanded. The prospect of company was appealing, notwithstanding his Sunday night custom. "No, that's silly," he said to no one in particular. "There is Greene to be read, and only one copy. You can share a meal, but not easily a novel."

"Is there a draft in this house? Why does it seem so cold

in here," Barrett exclaimed in exasperation. Putting his meal preparation aside, he walked through the dining room, around the corner into his now dark living room. Without turning on a light, he groused, "The blasted front door's open. Now how did I leave it unlatched?" he queried aloud, actually finding himself a bit relieved that there was a ready and natural explanation for the inimical atmosphere of his home.

Foster Barrett returned to his kitchen by the same route he had taken. This was the long way round to his front door, for his house was built like a square, and one could reach the kitchen more directly through a hallway from the living room. But going by way of the dining room to the front door enabled him to check the main fenestration of the house and the security of the sliding door off the dining room as well.

Foster Barrett performed the finishing touches on his meal's preparation. Taking a five-inch Solingen steel knife from its rack, he cut up some parsley to garnish the red snapper that had just been taken from the oven. This final task of aesthetics done, he placed the cutting implement on the counter and brought his main course and salad to the dining room table. As he brought the edibles into the next room, the sound of Vivaldi became more acute to his senses. For the first time in the evening he realized that he was taking in, and not just hearing, the music. His mood had changed. The coldness he had experienced earlier was gone, as was the sense of loneliness. The music, the cooking, the anticipated reading—the civility these things represented to Barrett—helped him put his moroseness and even his thoughts of the day's events behind him. The suicide of the economist, the unpleasantness with the press, these things should pass quickly, he thought. The bone china and sterling silver gleamed up at him as he lowered himself into his chair. He positioned himself at the end of the table, with his back to the kitchen. This way he could take full advantage of the room's acoustics.

Barrett knew only for an instant the advantage this also gave to the one who earlier had entered his front door. The meal on which he had lavished so much attention would not be enjoyed. Graham Greene would go unread. Foster Barrett had taken only a mouthful of the red snapper when he noticed a shadow cross the side of the table where he sat. Startled, he turned in his chair toward the kitchen, only to catch the glint from the Solingen steel blade as it was being thrust downward toward his chest. There was, again, no time to reflect, no time to muse.

The death of Morrison Bell had at first baffled the police. There did not seem to be a clear motive. The usual presupposition of the police, that the murderer was an addict looking for household valuables to fence, seemed implausible in this instance. Mrs. Bell and the police had made a search of the house and from the observation of both no valuables seemed to be missing, even though the back door to the house and the sliding door into the bedroom were unlocked, and the latter had been found open. Nor were any items missing from the garage, though nothing of significant value was stored there. Moreover the coroner had estimated that Bell had been dead for over an hour before his family returned home and discovered his body. This would have given a thief ample time to ransack the house.

The murder of the Harvard mathematician sent shock waves through Cambridge. There were the immediate neighborhood effects. Those close to the Bell residence became even more concerned with their own security. And of course many knew and liked the Bells as neighbors and felt sorrow over the tragedy that had befallen the family. Over the weekend, as the news of his death reached his colleagues and students in the Mathematics department, his slaying was a constant topic of conversation and speculation. For the handful of graduate students working directly under him, there was a double loss. On one level they mourned the death of their teacher. On another they fretted over its implications for the completion of their research and dissertations. For his immediate family, for the police, and for many who knew him only casually the big question was, "why?"

There were any number of possible explanations. For although Morrison Bell was widely admired, he was not universally loved. His high standards in his work applied not only to himself but to others. And those who did not measure up in his eyes often felt the lash of his criticisms. The wounds he left were deep and did not heal quickly. In some they festered, as the police were to learn through their inquiries.

Notwithstanding the possible motives that many might have in hoping for the demise of Morrison Bell, the police dismissed all of them almost immediately upon learning of the brutal killing of Foster Barrett. When the news was broken, following the discovery on Monday morning of his body by his cleaning woman, fear swept the Cambridge community. Two murders of members of the Harvard faculty within two days suggested the possibility that a madman was loose. The locksmiths of the area were inundated with inquiries about security devices and companies selling alarm systems were preparing to do a brisk business.

The Spearmans got the news of the death of Foster Barrett from a radio newscast. Henry had sat down to his noon meal, and as was his custom when he was home for lunch, he tuned to the twelve o'clock news. When the commentator announced the discovery of Barrett's remains, Spearman at first thought surely there was a bizarre mistake: that the announcer was reporting the old news of Morrison Bell's murder. But that illusion was soon dispelled when the details were recited.

"Henry, I think you're in danger. You were on the committee with both of them." Pidge had turned pale and looked uncertainly at her husband from across their kitchen table.

"I think not, Pidge. The only connection between Barrett and Bell is that they both voted against Dennis Gossen. That information has somehow been made known to the public. Under the rules, I was not permitted to vote. And that too is well known to those who read the newspaper accounts. Besides it's common knowledge that I was Gossen's strongest supporter. It is probable that what's motivating this killer is revenge. And if so, we're in no danger. Those who have something to fear are Valerie Danzig and Denton Clegg. I hope the police understand that and are giving them protection."

"But why would someone be taking revenge for Dennis Gossen's suicide?"

"I didn't know Dennis Gossen well enough to attempt an answer to that question. It could be anyone who cared for him a great deal. Perhaps a relative or a close friend. Who knows? In cases like this it is better to ask 'what' questions and not 'why' questions."

Henry Spearman got up from the table and walked toward the kitchen phone. He planned to call his friend to advise him to take precautionary measures. But before he could place his hand on the receiver the instrument rang. "Hello, Henry?" a familiar voice said.

"What a coincidence, Denton. I was just about to call you. I'm sure you've heard the news about Foster Barrett. I wanted to call to urge you to take every precaution these days. In my view, someone has a vendetta, and if so you and Danzig are . . . "

"That's what I was calling you about, Henry. It's obvious that you haven't heard even later news. Valerie and I are safe. I've been in contact with the police since early this morning. Ten minutes ago they arrested Melissa Shannon for the murder of Foster Barrett and Morrison Bell."

14
Wednesday, March 20
Friday, March 22
Monday, March 25

The Commonwealth of Massachusetts v. *Melissa Shannon.* Judge Manning Baxter did not have to look at his courtroom docket to be reminded that today he would be presiding over one of the most celebrated criminal cases of his career. As Associate Justice of the Superior Court for Middlesex County, he had been assigned the murder trial of Melissa Shannon. He was relieved that the jury selection process was over. This already had taken two trial days. Now the trial of the defendant could begin in earnest. As he donned his robes to enter the courtroom, Baxter reminded himself that his audience today would not be the ordinary collection of plaintiffs and defendants and legal counsel, plus the usual courtroom crowd—along with an occasional civics class come to watch justice roll.

Judges knew that murder trials attracted an unsavory element of society that was titillated by murderers and fascinated by the details of violent crime. The "courtroom ghouls" should be out in force today, Baxter thought, as his fingers made his tie more comfortable beneath the protective front of his robe. There would be other intrusive spectators who would crowd in today to see firsthand a woman who would avenge by murder her lover's suicide. Judge Baxter's colleagues had told him to expect as well visitors from the Harvard academic community: faculty colleagues and friends of the victim and members of the administration. They would be present to witness the wheels of justice and no doubt hope for a conviction and sentence that would deter any more such deadly behavior, of which they might bear the unfortunate brunt.

Representing the Commonwealth would be Dorothy Nolan, the assistant district attorney for Middlesex County. She had been appointed to her position three years ago by the district attorney, after her graduation from law school and a clerkship with a federal judge. Like most lawyers who serve in the office of the district attorney, she had political goals higher than her current career post. Winning this case would elevate her reputation as an advocate and would not be a hindrance to those aspirations. The conviction of Melissa Shannon could be a stepping-stone to a higher office. This alone would have provoked her to prepare for today's trial with particular diligence. But, in addition, Nolan believed in her case. The evidence was circumstantial, and that was her greatest litigative obstacle. But in her own mind she was convinced that Shannon had killed Morrison Bell, the crime for which the defendant was about to be tried. The district attorney had decided there was a stronger case on the Bell murder than the killing of Barrett. Hence the decision to prosecute that crime first.

Mrs. Nolan's principal adversary at the Cambridge courthouse was James Reilly, an attorney with a small law firm in Cambridge that specialized in criminal work. Reilly was highly regarded by the local bar. Prominent cases can attract good attorneys, notwithstanding in this instance Melissa Shannon's modest financial means. Reilly had predicted to his colleagues that a victory was probable. He came close to bragging that Melissa Shannon would be set free. An acquittal would make him few friends among the police and the Bell family, but it would be valuable publicity, better than any paid advertisement, for the prowess of his firm. Moreover, after spending much time with Melissa Shannon, Reilly was persuaded of her innocence.

Henry Spearman had at first decided he would not attend the trial. His mid-semester commitments at Harvard were heavy, and he was preparing to go to California to give a paper at UCLA and Stanford; on his return he was scheduled to testify on Capitol Hill before the Joint Economic Committee. Moreover he was behind in the writing of his monthly column. But Calvin Weber had talked Spearman into attending, at least on the day Denton Clegg was expected to testify.

The Middlesex County courthouse is one of the tallest and most contemporary structures in the city of Cambridge. The building had opened in the 1970s under a cloud of scandal and controversy regarding financial irregularities in its construction. But by the time the cost of the elegant furnishings had faded from the media's memory, the marble and teakwood began to evoke thoughts of appreciation among the area residents. The building's courtrooms, semicircular in their dimensions, were more attuned to acoustical principles than judicial traditions. Members of the Middlesex County bar took a measured pride in the facility and believed it contrasted favorably with the stodgier trappings of the judiciary across the river in Boston.

There was only one person attending the trial who did not have to travel to the courthouse building. This was Melissa Shannon. To maximize the security of the prisoners, the jail occupied the top floors of the courthouse building. A walk down a protected corridor and a trip on a specially secured, limited-use elevator took Melissa Shannon from her cell to her trial. No travels outside were necessary.

"Ever been in court before, Henry?" Calvin Weber asked

casually as the two of them stood outside the courtroom awaiting admittance with the other spectators. They were joined by Denton Clegg, who was to be a witness for the prosecution.

"Only once, years ago when I was an assistant professor. And I must say, my testimony did not meet with much success."

"Why's that?" Clegg asked with the interest of one soon to take the stand.

"Too much economics, and too early." Spearman answered. "I'm told my testimony might be better received now."

"Because you're better known, of course," Clegg hazarded.

"No, not because *I'm* better known. Because *economics* is better known. There's been a revolution in the teaching of law, as you may know. And economic analysis has provoked the revolution. Are you aware that every major law school now has an economist on its faculty? All this has been marvelous for the demand for economists. Some of our best graduate students in economics now seriously consider appointments at law schools. And woe betide the undergraduate who enters Harvard Law, and many other places now, ignorant of microeconomic analysis. At one time lawyers had to learn rhetoric; now they had best learn cost curves." Spearman said all this, not hiding his pleasure at what he was reporting to his colleagues.

"You obviously knew all there was to know about cost curves, Henry, back when you said you testified. But you said you weren't successful as a witness. Did you get tripped up on cross-examination? That's what I've been told to beware of," Clegg responded.

"I wasn't so much tripped up as my testimony was never understood. I was asked by an attorney to testify in a personal injury case where a mother had been struck by a drunk driver, and as a result of injuries she was unable to function as a housewife for almost a year. Her husband had to hire help at home and paid over five thousand dollars—which was a lot of money then. The driver's insurance firm offered to pay the five thousand, arguing that was the monetary value of the housewife's services for the year. I was called as an expert witness to evaluate that figure."

"Well, wasn't the amount fair?" Weber asked, peering down at his friend. "I mean, if that's what the fellow paid out . . . "

"I can't say if it was fair or not, but it certainly did not match the value of this particular woman's services as a housewife. One thing I hadn't told you, but I certainly made clear during the trial, is that this particular woman was a CPA, a certified public accountant, though she chose not to work as one at the time of the accident. I estimated that CPAs of her training and experience made ten thousand dollars a year. That amount, not the five thousand, was the value to this family of the woman's services as a housewife. Now that's just elementary economics. But it sailed by the court's understanding, I'm afraid."

Spearman looked at his two friends. Their cryptic expressions caused him to press on. "The court looked at cost like an accountant would. It simply asked, what did the husband have to pay out? The economist looks at cost—even the beginning student, mind you—as the highest valued opportunity forgone. The cost of anything is the most desirable alternative you give up. And for this woman, that was ten thousand dollars. As a housewife, she and her family had agreed to forgo ten thousand dollars—precisely the income she could have made as a CPA. That's what she was worth to them at home. And that's what they should have received for the loss of her services. But the judge claimed he could not understand my testimony. Try as hard as I did, I could not persuade the court. And the family only got the five thousand." Spearman paused. "And I never testified again as an expert witness—though goodness knows a number of my colleagues in the economics department do, in all sorts of cases. Frankly, I've heard that some of the more traditional lawyers who haven't retooled are rather bitter over the way their turf has been invaded by economists."

"I'll shed no tears for them," Calvin Weber volunteered. "You won't find many people in my, shall I say, peer group, who are fond of lawyers. I've always admired what Dr. Samuel Johnson said about the breed."

"And what was that? I'll show my ignorance," Clegg said with a smile.

"Johnson was in a group of men who didn't all know each other. One of them left. A fellow who remained asked Johnson if he knew who that person was. And Johnson said, 'I do not care to speak ill of any man behind his back, but I believe the gentleman was an attorney.'" Spearman and Clegg both chuckled at the mot. For Clegg, it was a welcome respite from the tension he felt about testifying.

"Well, it's too late to learn economics," Clegg said, noting that the bailiff was permitting entrance to the courtroom. "Got any other advice for me?"

"Tell the truth, the whole truth, and nothing but the truth," Weber quipped.

The courtroom was called to order as Judge Baxter entered and the case was called for trial. Spearman watched impassively as the prosecution and defense attorneys made their opening statements. In her statement Dorothy Nolan stressed how the prosecution had the burden of proving Melissa Shannon guilty beyond all reasonable doubt. Throughout the presentation, her voice was medium pitched, carefully modulated, and strong. She spoke to the jury, not at them. Nolan had decided it was strategic to be forthright with the fact that most of the Commonwealth's case was circumstantial. But she argued forcefully that evidence was often circumstantial and yet conclusive. And she cautioned the jury against believing otherwise.

James Reilly then announced to the jury that he could be very brief in his opening statement. He said that the prosecution had made his statement for him: that Melissa Shannon had to be proved guilty beyond a reasonable doubt and that the jury, at the close of this case, would have doubts even as to why the Commonwealth would proceed against his client, who was already sorrowing over the loss of her fiancé, on the basis of such shaky evidence. He considered it strategic to be candid about the weakest part of his defense: that no one had been with or seen his client at the time of Bell's death. Shannon lived alone, and she would testify, Reilly explained, that she had slept in that morning because she was not scheduled to work and had not slept well the previous two nights.

Dorothy Nolan then began her case in chief. Standing beside the table that held her papers and exhibits, her beige wool suit complementing tastefully her brown hair, the assistant district attorney called her first witnesses: the county coroner and then the police officer who had arrested Melissa Shannon. As he watched Nolan, Weber thought it appropriate that Morrison Bell's murder trial was being prosecuted by someone who was as fastidious in matters of grooming as Bell had been.

This part of the trial had been like a play or television drama for most of the spectators, but it became more vivid with the coroner's direct testimony. His straightforward portrayal of the blow to Bell's head that had probably rendered him unconscious and the clinical description of the incision in Bell's chest that had killed him provoked visible emotions of sorrow or squeamishness among the spectators. Only the lawyers in the room seemed unmoved by the coroner's testimony.

"Are you able to identify the particular knife that you testified killed Professor Bell?" Reilly asked the coroner on cross-examination.

"No, as I mentioned in my direct testimony, we did not find the knife."

"No knife was in the body of the deceased?"

"That is correct."

"And so far as you know, the murder weapon, if it is a knife, has not been located?"

"No . . . I mean yes—that is, yes, it has never been located."

"Can you identify the type of knife that you testified took the life of the deceased?"

"No, not by brand, if that's what you mean. It was probably an ordinary kitchen knife, either a medium-length carving knife or one of the longer paring knives."

"Did you examine the kitchen knives owned by Melissa Shannon?"

"I did not personally, but they were taken to the lab and examined under my supervision."

"And what did you learn from them?"

"Nothing that would prove them to be the weapon. But there were knives in the defendant's possession that could have made the incision I described."

"I didn't ask you that, sir," Reilly retorted. "But since you volunteer, let me inquire if there are any knives in your kitchen that would have done the job as well?"

"Yes," the coroner paused, "and probably in your kitchen too, Mr. Reilly."

"But you did not find nor can you identify the knife you claimed killed Professor Bell?"

"No, I cannot."

Turning to the bench, Reilly said curtly, "Your honor, I have no further questions for this witness."

The police officer who had arrested Melissa Shannon was asked by the prosecution if the defendant was advised of her Miranda rights. The response from the officer was an assured affirmative. "And when you arrested Miss Shannon, officer, and had apprised her of her rights, can you tell us everything she told you."

"Objection! Hearsay," Reilly interjected, rising to make his point.

"Overruled," Baxter responded. "Knowledge of defendant's mental or physical state is an exception to the hearsay rule. You may sit down, Mr. Reilly."

The officer answered. "She said she wished the other two would soon be dead as well."

" 'The other two would soon be dead as well.' And did she say anything else?"

"Not much, she just repeated several times that she was glad the two professors were dead, and she wished the other two would join them."

"Did she identify whom she meant by the 'other two'?"

"Not by name, no."

"But she was adamant in what she said. Your memory is clear on this?"

"Oh yes, there was no doubt about it. That's what she said."

"Can you describe her demeanor, her emotional state at the time?"

"Yes, she was very distraught."

"Had she been drinking?"

"In my opinion, yes."

Reilly rose to cross-examine the officer. By this time, the distinction between the defense attorney's ensemble and his counterpart at the prosecution's table had been noticed by all spectators, except those oblivious to matters of attire and grooming. Reilly was wearing heavy rubber overshoes, though there was not a hint of rain that day, and he wore a fleecelike muffler under his jacket, even in the heat of the courtroom. He affected the look of Massachusetts' great trial lawyer of the past century, Rufus Choate. Choate had been careless in his attire but did not cross the line into slovenliness. Like Choate before him, Reilly consciously edged up to that same line. He did not want jurors to write him off as a loon, but he did want them to perceive that he was so taken by the cause of his client that matters of dress seemed irrelevant. It was as if his clothes were testifying, "Don't pay attention to me. I don't count. The cause of my client does."

The effectiveness of the officer's testimony was weakened somewhat by Reilly's drawing from him that it had been the officer's experience on more than one occasion to find that distraught people had not done what they claimed or meant what they said.

As the officer left the witness stand, Spearman and Weber both found themselves glancing across the arc of the courtroom to watch Valerie Danzig and Denton Clegg. Each of them must have thought often of the circumstances that led to Bell's and Barrett's deaths but had spared them the same fate.

Denton Clegg was called to the stand next and gave testimony as to the nature and steps of the promotion process at Harvard: why promotion to a tenured position was such a singularly important matter in the life of a great university and how monumental the decision often was to those individuals directly affected by it.

Clegg handled himself with an aplomb that was pleasing to the faculty and administration members present, and he seemed relaxed and ever mindful of opportunities to insert defenses and justifications for the procedures as he described them. Reilly's objections to Clegg's testimony were on the grounds of relevance. Over and again, he intoned, "Your honor, what does this have to do with proving anything about my client? We're not here to consider a young man's suicide. I thought we were here because my client has been charged with murder!"

On cross-examination Reilly lit into Dean Clegg about the leaked information of the voting on Gossen. Nolan objected on the grounds this was beyond the scope of Clegg's direct examination, but under Massachusetts' rules of evidence she expected that Baxter would permit cross-examination outside the topics of direct testimony. He did. Nolan knew this could work in her favor later. Reilly hammered away: "Are the results of the promotion and tenure committee's deliberations normally kept confidential?" "Have they always been in the past up until this year?" "Is it important to you that these votes be kept secret?" "How then do you account for them being made known?" "Was the breach a major one, in your opinion?" "Would students at Harvard have known the identity of those who voted against Gossen?" "Would townspeople have known?" "Could anyone who watched the news not have known?" "Was there anything unusual then about Melissa Shannon admitting to having this information?"

Clegg weathered this part of the cross-examination, and showed one of the traits that endeared him to the faculty when he told Reilly outright in response to a question, "Look, the breach in secrecy came from a committee I chaired. I do not believe it was a member of the committee who violated this trust. I fear the leak came from someone in my office who, in the excitement concerning Mr. Gossen's suicide, revealed the vote. Several people had access to that information. But Mr. Reilly, be that as it may, the buck stops with me in such matters. If you are looking for the person responsible for letting out the information about the negative votes of Bell and Barrett and Danzig, and myself for that matter, you can stop with me!"

"Dean Clegg, there is one other matter I want to ask you about," Reilly said, after a long consultation with the notes on the table before him. "I'm not a Harvard man, as I know Judge Baxter is. You'll have to be patient with my ignorance. Can you tell me, sir, if relations among faculty at Harvard are always harmonious?"

Clegg seemed surprised by the question. He thought before responding. "Harmonious is not the word I would choose. At times the faculty works together as a team—the P and T committee would be an example, I suppose. But it is in the nature of teaching and research that they are often done alone. There's no need for harmony."

"Perhaps you miss the point of my question. Let me rephrase it. Is there ever tension, distrust, jealousy among the learned staff at Harvard?"

"Well of course there is lively disagreement. Every great center of intellectual activity has this."

"I didn't ask about lively disagreement, Dean Clegg. I asked about jealousy—if I have to spell it out for you, hatred, intense dislike. Could faculty members like Morrison Bell, or Foster Barrett, make enemies in the course of their work? Can there be colleagues who would come to have an intense dislike of them?"

"Oh, that's possible, I suppose. I might not use the term 'enemy.' There are personality conflicts. Scholars are not people without emotions, I trust you know that, Mr. Reilly. Yes, we have our differences. But they are no cause for murder, if that's what you are suggesting."

"Dean Clegg, maybe you don't get out of the ivory tower very much, I don't know. But we have people killed on the streets in this town over differences about who got to a parking place first! Are the issues and conflicts that Professor Bell might encounter, as a faculty member, of less consequence than that?"

"Well you've unwittingly hit upon a sore point, Mr. Reilly. At most universities parking spaces are at such a premium that faculty members might kill to get one." Clegg turned his head slightly and smiled at the judge. "I'm jesting, of course, your honor. My point is that in intellectual communities the guiding principle is to settle differences by debate and discourse, not by way of violence."

When Clegg left the stand, Judge Baxter called a recess and Weber and Spearman found themselves in the hall talking with Valerie Danzig and Oliver Wu. Spearman had not spotted Wu during the trial and was surprised to see him at the courthouse since he had gathered from several observations in January that Bell and Wu were not friends.

"Are you persuaded she did it?" Wu asked of the threesome.

"All I know is that since they picked the woman up, I'm alive and not dead," Danzig replied. "The killings have stopped."

"It will take more than that to convince a jury," Wu responded. "I believe the fact that the killings have stopped is inadmissible evidence to the jury. That's to have no bearing on their decision. And remember this is not a Harvard jury. Pick any twelve people from the Cambridge population and you may get some who would like the murder of Harvard profs to continue."

"Well, I'll venture she gets off scot free," Weber asserted, surprising everyone.

"How can you deduce that so soon, Calvin?" Spearman inquired, for the economist knew he was not in a position to draw any conclusions at this point.

"Melissa Shannon has two things going for her—and that's all she needs. One is her sex. In America we don't allow our murderers to be women. Look at our literature, our film, our theatre. It happens so rarely as to be an aberration."

"And the second part of your reasoning?" Wu asked.

"She has a great attorney. And in Anglo-Saxon jurisprudence, that goes a long way in determining innocence. Do you remember Gilbert & Sullivan's *Trial by Jury*? There's a song that goes:

> All thieves who could my fees afford
> Relied on my orations,
> And many a burglar I restored
> to his friends and his relations.

Melissa Shannon will be restored, you wait and see."

"Hmmm," Spearman muttered. "Remember, Calvin, the

song refers to burglars being restored. It may be a different matter with murderers."

Spearman originally had thought he would return home following Clegg's testimony, but instead he joined several faculty members at a downtown eatery for lunch upon learning that the prosecution would call Christolph Burckhardt as its witness in the afternoon. After Clegg had left the witness stand, and before the luncheon recess, Dorothy Nolan called three witnesses, all close acquaintances of Melissa Shannon who were asked to testify about Shannon's relationship with Dennis Gossen. Each in turn described the couple's plan to marry. Nolan pressed them with questions that revealed their understanding of the importance of Gossen's promotion to Melissa Shannon. One of the witnesses indicated that a trip to Europe was in store for Gossen and Shannon as a result of the promotion and its attendant higher income. Another testified that the promotion would clinch their plans to purchase a home. All of them made clear that to Melissa as well as her fiancé a great deal rode on Gossen's promotion. The witnesses uniformly testified that Melissa Shannon was distraught by Gossen's death.

Reilly's cross-examination of these witnesses was brief. In effect, he got them to admit that it was not unnatural or peculiar to be distraught over the death of a future spouse. "Would they not feel the same way?" he asked. And each one volunteered that it was not extraordinary for a person to place great stock in the professional success of a spouse.

Every attorney, in preparing to examine a witness, hopes fervently for one thing: that there be no surprises. Thus far there had been no great surprises. Both attorneys had cause to be pleased with how the trial was proceeding. At 2 p.m., immediately after Wednesday's luncheon recess, the prosecutor called her last witness.

"Will Christolph Burckhardt please take the stand?"

To Spearman, the stamp merchant appeared older, his face more ashen, than he had ever seen him to be. His voice was unsteady as he was sworn in. Valerie Danzig, who had seated herself between Spearman and Weber for the afternoon session, commented to each of them how uncertain Burckhardt appeared—how ill at ease compared to the coroner, the police officer, Dean Clegg, and the acquaintances of Miss Shannon.

"Mr. Burckhardt," the prosecutor began, after the witness had been sworn in and his identity established, "I want to ask you several questions about Miss Melissa Shannon, the defendant in this trial. Do you know her personally?"

"Yes."

"Can you identify her in this courtroom?"

"Yes, that is she over there," the witness said, pointing his left index finger at the accused.

"And how do you know her?"

"She was my employee."

"And is that all?" Nolan probed.

"We were also friends."

"And what was the character of your friendship? By that I mean, was it amorous—or was it platonic—just friends—or what?"

Burckhardt hesitated and he did not respond immediately. Dorothy Nolan stood impassively, waiting for an answer to her question. The witness's eyes winced and he pursed his lips as he vainly held back the full force of the emotion he felt. His ashen face changed its hue, and it became red. His fingers nervously played with the armrests of the witness chair. Judge Baxter looked down at the man quizzically. "We were friends, good friends, that's all," he eventually replied.

Reilly tried to conceal his surprise at the witness's answer and demeanor by doodling on the yellow pad before him. Burckhardt's display of emotion had taken him aback.

"As friends, did you have occasion to notice anything about her attire?"

"On occasion, yes."

"Your honor, I want to use the Commonwealth's exhibit A, introduced earlier by Officer Vickers when he was on the stand."

"You may proceed," Baxter said, motioning to the exhibit lying on a table.

"Mr. Burckhardt, I'm showing you an item of apparel that was found in the hedge outside the home of Morrison Bell the day of his death. Can you identify this item?"

"It appears to be a woman's glove."

"And can you tell me if you have ever seen this glove before?"

Burckhardt paused again. His delay in responding was over a minute. To the spectators it seemed to be an hour. He looked over at the defendant with an expression of wistfulness. "I've seen it worn by Melissa Shannon. It is her glove."

Valerie Danzig turned to Calvin Weber and said, "You may be wrong in your prediction. Life does not always imitate art."

Weber, like everyone else, was surprised by the revelation of the glove's ownership.

"Now, Mr. Burckhardt, you indicated you were friends with Miss Shannon. That she was more than an employee. Did you ever see her socially?"

"Yes."

"More than once?"

"Yes."

"More than twice?"

"Yes, more than twice."

"Could I say 'frequently'?" Nolan asked.

"Regularly," Burckhardt responded.

"And during these occasions, were you aware that your friend and employee was engaged to be married?"

"Objection," Reilly's voice rang out.

"Sustained," Judge Baxter held.

"Mr. Burckhardt, in your relationships with Miss Shannon that were not professional, could you tell me the last time you escorted Miss Shannon somewhere, the last time you saw her socially?"

"Let me see. That would have been on January seventh. She was my consort at a party in honor of Dr. Clegg."

"And where did this take place? At the Clegg home?"

"No, it was at the home of a Dr. Spearman." Henry Spearman's back stiffened at the sound of his own name being mentioned in the trial. "I was asked to speak about a particular stamp that was being presented to Dr. Clegg that evening. It was only natural that Miss Shannon would go with me, since the evening involved philately."

"Did you know at that time Melissa Shannon was engaged . . . no, strike that, was Mr. Dennis Gossen, Miss Shannon's fiancé, present that evening?"

"Of course not," Burkhardt said, "Why should he be?"

"Let me ask the questions, Mr. Burckhardt," Nolan chided gently. "I gather your answer is a simple no. Could you tell me who was present."

"No, I can't identify everyone there."

"Let me try and help you then," Nolan said. "I take it Dean Denton Clegg was present."

"Yes, I said as much," Burkhardt replied testily.

"And was Professor Morrison Bell present that evening?"

"Yes."

"Did Melissa Shannon meet Professor Bell that evening?"

"Yes, she did."

"You know that for a fact?"

"Yes, I was with her. I met Bell myself for the first time. She talked with him more than I did. As I recall, they talked about birds. Mr. Bell spoke about actually caring for birds at his home. In his backyard as I recall. I didn't pay that much attention to their conversation. I stood by politely. Frankly, if a bird isn't on a stamp or a dinner plate, I don't find it of much interest."

"Did Miss Shannon meet Professor Foster Barrett that evening as well?"

John Reilly rose quickly to his feet. "Objection, your honor. Immaterial." The defense attorney was overruled and the witness was directed to answer the question.

"Yes, they met and talked at some length."

"Were you a part of the conversation?"

"Yes, we talked about our club. Barrett and I are members of the same club in Boston, though I did not know the man well. Oh yes, we also learned that we were each scheduled to be on the same voyage to England this spring. Or we would have been. We talked about the sailing. Just chitchat, that sort of thing."

"And Melissa Shannon was present during this conversation about your club. Did you talk about the club's dining schedule?"

"Yes, being bachelors we talked about the club being closed

on Sunday evenings. That is a failing of the club, from my standpoint. I don't like to cook for myself on the weekends. But Professor Barrett spoke of how he rather enjoyed cooking for himself that evening."

"Was anyone else present during this conversation? Or was it just the two of you?"

"There was another man with us. Name of Wu. I did not know him before; he's not a philatelist. He was not present during our conversation with Bell."

"Anyone else?"

"Not that I can recall."

"Mr. Burckhardt. This may be my last question. Have you seen or have you been with Melissa Shannon since that evening of January 7th?"

"I saw her that week—many times—at the store. But she left Friday as soon as the news came of the suicide. She was terribly upset, as one would imagine. Shocked is the better word. She didn't want to see anyone. Family or friends. I did try to call her over the weekend but never got through. To answer your question, I have not seen her since the morning of the 11th. Until today."

"Your honor, I have no other questions." And with that, Nolan announced that this ended the Commonwealth's case in chief.

The jury was excused as Judge Baxter entertained Reilly's motion to dismiss the case. From the bench he recited the evidence and held that the government had established a prima facie case. He told Mr. Reilly to be prepared to go ahead with his defense when the trial resumed the next day. At 4:30 p.m., the Superior Court for Middlesex County was adjourned.

Henry Spearman did not travel to the courthouse the following day to watch the continuation of the trial. But the local press gave major attention to the court proceedings and the economist listened with attention as Pidge relayed to him the news account of the completion of the trial.

"According to the morning paper, Miss Shannon was put on the stand and claimed she had been at home the morning that Bell was killed and that she had been terribly depressed. But listen to this part, Henry: she admitted that she had not seen anyone that morning, she couldn't remember having any phone calls, and she could not even identify a thing that was on television."

"What did she say about her glove?" Henry asked.

"She said that the glove was hers, but said she had lost it before. She claimed she had no idea how it got to Bell's house. She even denied that she had meant what she said to the police. But at least she confessed to having said it." Pidge Spearman picked up her cup of tea and began to scan the rest of the paper.

"Well, what is the result?" her husband asked.

"We won't know for a while. It says here the lawyers made their closing arguments to the jury and the jury is off deciding. I don't think it would take *me* too long."

The jury needed less than two hours on Monday before returning to the courtroom where Judge Baxter asked them if they had reached a verdict. Every eye in the courtroom was at that point fixed upon the jury's foreman, a middle-aged man who worked as a baker.

"Yes we have, your honor."

The jury found Melissa Shannon guilty of murder in the second degree. The conviction received the automatic penalty imposed by the Commonwealth of Massachusetts. When the academic community of Harvard learned that Melissa Shannon had been sentenced to life imprisonment in the penitentiary for the death of Morrison Bell, there was a measure of relief. Friends of Valerie Danzig and Denton Clegg, in particular, were happy, for they believed their friends were no longer in danger.

15
Sunday, June 9
Monday, June 10

"Hold it right there! Smile!" A flash of light. "That's it. Pass right on through." The photographer had caught the Spearmans by surprise. Henry looked up, expecting to be told he was at the wrong place. Pidge was adjusting the shoulder strap of her carry-on bag.

"Check the Photo Arcade tomorrow morning for the picture of you boarding the *QE2*." The Spearmans had just completed the trek up the gangplank of the *Queen Elizabeth 2*.

"Do you think we'll look good?" Henry asked.

"It won't be a Fabian Bachrach," Pidge replied. "And no one will mistake us for the Duke and Duchess of Windsor."

Contrary to the movies, you do not simply board a ship. First, there is the luggage ordeal. Without ceremony, baggage handlers take your suitcases and garment bags and begin piling them precariously on large dollies. Then, with no explanation or receipt given, the luggage disappears, leaving each passenger with the sinking feeling that the bags and their carefully selected contents will never be seen again.

Second, there are the waiting lines. A ship like the *QE2*, boarding hundreds of passengers for a single transatlantic crossing, will have long queues, as passengers must individually go through ticket, security, and passport checks.

And third, there is the confusion. United States citizens are expected to be in one place, British subjects elsewhere. Others have a separate processing track. Finding your own niche in the cavernous hubbub of Pier 84 on the Hudson River tested the mettle of even seasoned travelers.

"That lift will take you to Four Deck," a white-coated steward said in response to Pidge Spearman's inquiry.

"Straight a'ead, mum."

"Here it is," Henry Spearman said with relief, checking the number on the door against that on his travel record. The two entered their stateroom. Henry tapped his wife on the shoulder, and, smiling, pointed to the corner where their luggage had been stacked. They looked quickly through their room and decided that unpacking could wait. The ship was about to leave her berth, and the Spearmans did not want to miss being on deck as the *QE2* sailed from the New York harbor into the open sea.

The east and west shores of the Hudson River were as different as Jekyll and Hyde. As the great liner plied her way toward the Verrazano Narrows, passengers looking portside saw the glistening skyscrapers of Manhattan, anchored at the south by the twin towers of the World Trade Center. Even on a balmy Sunday afternoon, the city exuded an aura of financial dynamism. Travelers on starboard witnessed the industrial side of the nation's economy. Factories, refineries, smokestacks, warehouses—many of them in decaying condition—lined the New Jersey shoreline. Anchoring the industrial complex was the Maxwell House coffee plant in Hoboken, with its gargantuan tilted cup, perhaps as an offering to King Kong who might want a coffee break on his way to Manhattan to scale a skyscraper.

New York was the greater attraction and hundreds of travelers lined the deck rails portside to take departing photographs, enjoy the scenery, and savor the prospect of an ocean voyage. The Spearmans had positioned themselves early enough on Upper Deck overlooking the bow to take in both perspectives, and in doing so Henry Spearman was reminded of Thorstein Veblen's distinction between finance and industry. To Veblen, industry was the source of human wellbeing in that it was responsible for making goods; finance, on the other hand, which was responsible for making money, reaped most of the rewards. To Veblen, the financial side was not only sterile but a hindrance to economic development. The dichotomy was not one Spearman found useful since he believed that factors of production, whether financial or industrial, were equally productive at the margin. Nevertheless, the stark contrast between New Jersey and New York gave Veblen's distinction a kind of surface plausibility.

"Ah, Professor and Mrs. Spearman! I knew that you would be on board, but what a pleasant improbability that I would see you so soon out of port. This is actually my favorite part of the voyage. No matter how many times I go to Europe on business, I never lose the thrill of seeing the skyline of New York City pass before my eyes. Is this your first crossing?" Christolph Burckhardt appeared beside the Spearmans wearing a black raincoat belted at the waist and a natty straw hat.

"Actually, we've never sailed to Europe. On our previous visits, we flew," Pidge Spearman replied.

"Then you have a real treat in store for you. I never fly. An ocean liner is a most civilized way to bridge the continents."

"I'm surprised that time allows you to travel by ship," Henry Spearman observed.

"In my case that is really not a problem. Stamp auctions are announced well in advance so I use the time on board to plan my bidding stategy."

"May I assume you divulge all your secrets in your book?

I've brought it along for shipboard reading. In fact, I've already dipped into it."

Burckhardt looked flustered. "Oh Professor Spearman, I'm flattered you would want to read my book. But I'm afraid you will find it a bit dull. It's only the reminiscences of an old man and his stamps. I think you'll find horribly pedestrian my tracing of the history of the prices of famous stamps. And the good stories, I think you've heard me tell—such as the time I outbid the Weil brothers for the Hawaiian missionaries, or how I got taken on some fake inverted biplanes, and how I let some of the great rarities get away from me."

"None of that sounds dull to me. Good stories always bear repeating, and besides, there's a vast difference between hearing a story and reading one when I have time to savor it. And as for prices, well, for me prices are never boring. They are always reflections of underlying economic reality. Believe me, reading your book will not be a waste of my time."

"But as I understand it from your Dean, this isn't exactly a pleasure cruise for you, is it?" Don't you have to, what is the expression, sing for your supper? I understand there are dozens of Harvard alumni on board who have reverted to their student days. And you're scheduled to be one of their professors, are you not?"

"Oh, you mean *Harvard at Sea*. I suppose Denton told you about that? Actually, I will be engaged for part of the voyage giving some lectures. But they will not require extensive preparation. And I imagine the Harvard grads who have signed up for the course would not want it any other way. I don't expect them to be burning the midnight oil—at least over their reading assignments."

Spearman was distracted by an arm around his shoulder placed there by a gregarious Calvin Weber. "Calvin! I'm glad you made it," the economist said looking up to greet his friend. "You remember Christolph Burckhardt, don't you? He spoke so graciously at our home last winter—at the Clegg occasion."

"Oh yes, I certainly do," Weber responded, shaking the philatelist's hand firmly. "Are you participating in *Harvard at Sea* like Henry and me?"

"Ah, I wish I were. But being neither scholarly enough to be on your faculty nor fortunate enough to have been a student, I'm simply a businessman going to work. My plans are to attend some auctions in London and Paris where some rarities are going on the block. So in a sense this is a working voyage for the three of us, isn't it?"

"Well, I'd put it in the category of 'nice work if you can get it,' as the old song goes," Weber chuckled. In exchange for a first-class passage, I am expected to give three lectures on English literature. The rest of the time you'll find me in a deck chair."

"Now Calvin, don't be so modest. If you're like Henry, you put in many hours preparing for those lectures. I know I didn't see my husband for three days while he was getting ready," Pidge Spearman interposed.

"Nevertheless, it's a good deal," Weber replied.

"In that case," Burckhardt said, "I should imagine that all of your colleagues would like to be instructors in this program. The two of you must be very special to have been selected by the alumni."

"The alumni had little to do with our selection," Henry Spearman said. "Except indirectly. They delegated that responsibility to your friend Denton Clegg, asking him only to be sure that a cross section of the college was included. Denton decided those criteria were fulfilled by the professors you met at our home last January. So you may see some familiar faces on board. Valerie Danzig, the psychologist, is here; so is Oliver Wu of Sociology; and Sophie Ustinov from the Chemistry department. And Denton is giving some lectures too, I believe. You already know more of the faculty than many of the students."

"Yes, I know them, but through circumstances that are painful for me. I also met your two colleagues who were killed—and I'm afraid, though it is still difficult for me to believe, that I introduced them to their murderer that night."

"Now Christolph," Henry Spearman said, "you must put that thought from your mind. No one holds you in any way responsible for that."

"I hate to interrupt, but I believe our ship is about to collide with a bridge." Calvin Weber's arm was pointed toward the span over the Verrazano Narrows. From their vantage point on Upper Deck, it appeared as though the world's largest liner was about to collide with the world's largest suspension bridge.

"No cause for alarm. We'll clear with plenty of room to spare," Burckhardt responded. His judgment was confirmed almost immediately by an announcement from the bridge. The P.A. system crackled. "Those of you observing our approach to the Verrazano Narrows Bridge will be experiencing an optical illusion. Passengers might believe that our ship will not fit under the span of the bridge. Let me assure you she will. Our funnel will clear quite easily, ladies and gentlemen."

And it did.

"It's getting chilly out here. Quite a change from an hour ago." Pidge Spearman was hugging herself against the gusty breeze that swept over the ship as the bow emerged from under the other side of the bridge. "I think we're both more suitably dressed for the harbor than the sea," Henry Spearman responded to his wife. "Perhaps this would be a good time to go below and do a little exploring. And also get our table assignment. We'll probably see all of you later this evening."

Entering the ship, the Spearmans encountered a tangle of passageways that skirted Tables of the World, the dining room for transatlantic-class passengers. They emerged midships at the Players' Club Lounge, a rectangular area adjoining the ship's theatre. Slot machines lined the walls of the lounge and aft was the ship's casino, its gambling tables arranged in an oval pattern in the center of the room. Exiting, the couple passed through the Photo Arcade on the port side, which fed into a corridor adjacent to the Double Room nightclub. Circling the dance floor, they passed one of the QE2's libraries.

They stopped to join others who were looking blankly at a "You Are Here" sign on the wall next to an elevator. "The shops are on Boat Deck; that's one flight up," they overheard someone say. A quick climb brought them to the next level, where they entered a short passageway leading to a pair of French doors. Peering through the panes, they saw a plush carpeted interior with ten overstuffed chairs and a handful of desks. "Here's where I'll be spending some of my time. What a wonderful room for reading," Henry Spearman remarked.

"Well, at least I'll know where to find you when I want you," Pidge smiled.

They turned in the direction of the ship's stern, where a long corridor took them to the Shopping Arcade.

Most of the stores in the arcade ran in two rows along the inside of the QE2. There were two shops centered at each end of the arcade. Passengers could walk up and down the interior of Boat Deck and window-shop as if on a commercial boulevard. A person could not cross over directly from a shop on one side to a store on the other because of a large interior hole in the deck that went much of the length of the arcade. In the evening passengers could gather at the railing around this oval hole and look down to the dance floor of the Double Room nightclub one deck below.

"Isn't that Valerie Danzig?" Henry asked, peering over his spectacles. "Yes, I believe it is." The Spearmans walked around several groups of milling passengers and approached the eminent psychologist, who was examining the watches on display in a jewelry store. Danzig saw their reflection in the shop window. "Hi there, what's new?" She turned to greet them.

"What's new?" Henry replied. "Well, we just saw New York and New Jersey. Is that enough new for one day?" Pidge looked embarrassed. "Have you had a chance to look over the shops? Anything interesting?"

"Well, I have been looking for something that I couldn't find in Boston and didn't get a chance to look for in New York. I'm hoping to add to my collection of glass figurines. I indulge myself by adding one statuette each year. Right now I'm only window-shopping and was about to stop even that. We were told not to be tardy in registering for a dinner table. Have you two done that already?"

"No, we've been exploring the ship. But thanks for the reminder," Henry said. "I think we should tend to that little matter now."

"Good morning, ladies and gentlemen. This is the Officer of the Watch speaking. The seas are moderate with a low swell. The weather is cloudy, fine and clear." Henry Spearman was awake but still in his bunk as he strained to hear the

weather report being given outside their stateroom over the
QE2's loudspeaker. He got up and began dressing. "It's going
to be good sailing today," he said, noticing his wife awakening.

Bending over in front of their stateroom door, Henry Spearman retrieved two small periodicals that had been slipped
under it in the early morning hours. One was the ship's daily
newspaper, the *QE2 Express*, which gave a capsule account
of the world's news as well as human interest stories from
on board. Each day's version of "A Festival of Life on QE2"
described the times and locations of shipboard activities.
Movies, bridge, exercise, a piano concert, arts and crafts, bingo,
trap shooting, a golf clinic, a floral display class—these were
available to passengers who wanted more than rest and ocean
scenery. Henry Spearman's lecture for the Alumni Association
would occupy his morning, but he and Pidge mapped out
activities for the rest of the day. They agreed not to miss
Captain Lawrence Corbett's cocktail party for first-class passengers in the Queen's Room. They expected this would be
a pleasant occasion before their second dinner on the ship.

Henry Spearman was taking the afternoon sun on Sports
Deck. Wrapped in one of the ship's blue woolen rugs, he
settled into a deck chair. His duties for *Harvard at Sea* had
been completed for the day, and this was his last chance to
enjoy the good weather before getting ready for tonight's
activities. He thought his lecture had gone well, although he
couldn't be certain. Alumni have a tendency to hold professors
in more awe than they did when they were enrolled as undergraduates. They were all extremely polite, applauding when
the lecture ended and coming up afterward to express their
appreciation.

"Is this chair taken?" A gray-bearded, well-coiffed gentleman motioned to the empty deck chair adjacent to Spearman's. "No, I don't believe so," Spearman replied. "And there's a spare rug on the chair over here. May I hand it to you?"

"No thanks. I'm quite comfortable as is. This muffler is all I need."

Henry Spearman's eyes turned to focus on a wide, beige scarf the man was wearing. "I don't believe I've seen a piece of attire quite like that—incidentally, my name is Henry Spearman."

"The economist? I've read several of your columns. My name is Sidney Madison. I'm with Blaine-Madison, the department store. You asked about my muffler. Isn't it glorious?" He leaned over so Spearman could feel the fabric. "It's actually made from the neck hairs of the Himalayan ibex. The hairs stick on branches as the goats forage for food. It's called shahtoose. As an economist, you can probably appreciate that it is very rare."

"And I would predict, therefore, rather expensive. I hope you will forgive this particular economist being gauche, but may I ask the price?"

"It's not something you'll find in the typical clothing store. Shahtoose costs $1,500 a yard. My buyers tell me it's the most expensive fabric in the world. But you know, speaking of expense, tell me this—as an economist now—how can this ship keep going? I've wondered since we got on. I've even done some rough calculations. Just back of an envelope figuring, mind you. But I think they're reasonable estimates. With all the fuel, provisions, and staffing—not to mention the cost of the ship—how can Cunard justify operating it?"

"By not mentioning the cost of the ship."

"I beg your pardon?"

"By not mentioning the cost of the ship. That is, by ignoring the fixed costs: such as the vessel's depreciation, interest to its bondholders, salaries to the corporate executives of Cunard, and the like. They have to pay those whether the *QE2* goes to England this week or not. As long as what the passengers pay to reach Southampton—for their tickets and all they spend on board—covers the cost of operating the ship for this one crossing, Cunard comes out ahead."

"How could that be? They still have to pay interest to their bondholders."

"But they have to pay their bondholders anyway—unless they default. If the revenues from this crossing exceed *by only one dollar* the cost of the ship's fuel and its food and the wages of its staff, that is a dollar Cunard has that it would not possess if it did not run the *QE2*. Take your store in downtown Dallas. Under what conditions would you close it down? Not if you couldn't pay interest to your creditors. What good would closing the store do? You *still* couldn't pay interest to your creditors. But you *would* close your store if its sales didn't cover the wages of your clerks or the cost of maintaining your inventory. Because then you wouldn't have those costs. That's why they're called variable costs. Interest is a fixed cost because it doesn't disappear if you close the store down. Now of course you wouldn't be able to do that forever. Eventually you would have to cover all of your costs. But in the short run, you can keep going."

For the next hour Spearman and Madison exchanged views on the nation's economy, and Spearman was reluctant to leave for his afternoon exercise at the ship's gymnasium. "A fascinating discussion, Professor. I hope to see you again. If you and your wife ever get to Dallas, I'd love to give you a tour of the store."

"Good evening, Mr. and Mrs. Spearman, glad to have you with us." An aide to Captain Corbett had just taken the Spearmans' name from them and introduced the couple to the Master of the *QE2*. The line of first-class passengers, all formally attired, extended through the forward portside entrance to the Queen's Room as the travelers queued up to meet the Captain and be photographed at the precise moment of the handshake. Captain Corbett photographed well in his white uniform, his black hair slicked down, and his thin physique gave him the patrician look of a true English sea captain. The Spearmans and others moved quickly through the line as Corbett glibly answered with stock responses questions he had heard over and again.

The Spearmans met several other guests and encountered Oliver Wu standing alone at an hors d'oeuvres table. Spearman and Wu compared notes about their morning lectures until their conversation was stopped by the introduction of the chief officers of the *QE2*'s staff. Everybody got a mention, from the Chief Medical Officer to the Staff Captain. At the close of the introductions Corbett told the assembled guests, "Thank you, ladies and gentlemen. On behalf of Cunard Lines and the entire crew, it is a pleasure and privilege to have you on board. Welcome. The weather should be smooth and there should be no problem arriving on time. Thank you."

On the heels of the Captain's cocktail party, the Spearmans followed the herd of other guests to the Columbia Room, one of the three dining areas for first-class passengers. It was the largest of them and was marked by its tasteful appointments and large windows, providing an expansive view of the sea.

There are three important things passengers learn about

dining on an ocean liner. One, meals are important, and not just for nourishment or because the food is excellent—which it is. Shipboard life for many, even after only one or two days out, can seem confining and patterned. Excellent meals of astonishing variety break the monotony. Two, waiters are important. If a passenger is a beluga caviar fan, the waiter can see to it that the portions are extra large at every sitting; in addition he can report what looks good in the kitchen and what should be avoided. Three, table companions are important. A passenger is assigned the same table for the duration of the crossing. Being stuck with meal table partners who are irritating, boring, or just plain obnoxious can come close to ruining an entire voyage. The safest course is to select a table no larger than will accommodate the travelers with whom the passenger desires company.

The Spearmans had decided to dine alone. They had a small table against the aft bulkhead that gave them a view toward the starboard windows. Henry and Pidge studied the offerings. An eleven-course dinner was available, though few passengers had the capacity for all of them at a single sitting. "It was hard to decide," Pidge responded. "But I think I'm ready to order." Pidge had a "Tempting Starter," skipped something "From the Cauldrons," tried some turbot "From the Seas and Rivers," passed up the "Farinaceous," ordered Duck *à l'orange* from "The Main Fare," refused even to consider anything "From the Grill," although buttered garden peas from "The Accompaniments" sounded fine. "The Cold Table" was dismissed without a second thought, but tossed greens from "Crisp and Fresh" would do nicely; and she would wait awhile to decide on "Sweet Revelations." After all this she predicted that she would forgo the meal's concluding platter of British and continental cheeses. After Henry Spearman had placed his order, the two of them settled in to enjoy their second evening at sea.

As the Spearmans were waiting for their desserts, Sophie Ustinov appeared dragging a chair from an adjacent table that had just been vacated. "Darlinks, what a relief to see you! I asked my waiter to serve me my dessert here. I knew you wouldn't mind. I couldn't stay at my table another minute. I see you did the right thing and got a small one. At my table there is a man who—you would not believe it—talks nonstop, I mean not even a pause for a breath. What he's talking about I do not know; I stopped listening after the soup. I take that back. There's one thing that stops his blabbing. His big black cigar, which he smoked at the table. —Yes, darlink, put it right down here, thank you for bringing it—He smoked it till I asked him to stop. But then he talked more than ever. I don't know what was worse, the talk or the smoke."

The Spearmans looked on with sympathetic expression. "That's terrible, Sophie. Perhaps you can get the maître d' to find you another table."

"Believe me, I'll tell him. But do you think it's possible? The dining room looks so crowded."

"He can probably come up with something. This is not the only first-class dining room. Anyway, you must give it a try." Pidge was encouraging.

Sophie spooned the last of her Bavarian strawberry cream pie from her plate. "Delicious. But too heavy. On top of everything else, I don't even know why I'm eating it. How many courses are there? Ten, twelve, there must be a dozen. In Cambridge, I would never order so much. If I have an appetizer, would I get soup? Never. If I have fish, do I then get veal? Ridiculous. And the pasta. Did you two get pasta? That's a meal in itself. But me, like a fool, I ate it."

"You're no fool, Sophie. You're behaving quite rationally. It makes perfect sense to eat more here than in Cambridge," Henry Spearman responded.

"Sure, because the food's so good."

"No, it's not a question of quality. There are excellent restaurants in our area. But even holding the quality of the restaurant constant, you'd still want to eat more on the ship because of relative prices. Here everything in the dining room is at zero price."

"Sure because *Harvard at Sea* pays," she said.

"No, not because the Alumni Association pays. Even if you had paid full fare for this crossing, an extra portion of any item on the menu would cost you nothing. In most restaurants of course that's not the case. Before you decide whether to order the pasta, you'd look at the price. If the satisfaction you get from the pasta is greater than the satisfaction from the money you give up to get it, you place the order. You do the same thing here, except the price is zero. So as long as your enjoyment of the pasta is greater than the price, you select it. Therefore you select pasta if it yields only a tiny amount of satisfaction. Any amount greater than zero in fact. Or in economic jargon you keep eating until the marginal utility of another bite is zero. At that point you would be in equilibrium."

"I think I'd also weigh three hundred pounds," Sophie responded.

"In that case," Spearman said with a twinkle in his eye, "you'd not only have a considerable consumer's surplus in you, but everyone could see it sticking out as well."

16
Wednesday, June 12

Dinner was over. The four dining rooms had emptied and the passengers scattered throughout the ship. Their priorities differed: many of them preferred the new Hollywood film showing in the theatre; others the casino for roulette, blackjack, and slot machines; a few wanted the thrill of a mid-Atlantic telephone call to friends back home; still others window-shopped the svelte retail stores in the arcade; nightclubbing was the choice of the lion's share. The bulletin of daily events, "A Festival of Life on QE2," had announced a 1920s night in the Double Room for transatlantic class. For travelers in first class there was late-night dancing and soft lights in the Queen's Room.

But none of these attracted Henry Spearman. The after-dinner hours were his favorite time on board. The evening repast in the Columbia Room was exquisite, and the economist had eaten heartily during the day and exercised too little. His daily swim in the saltwater pool, his brisk walks on the prom-enade deck, and his time in the exercise room did not come close to offsetting the caloric intake of the ship's Lucullan feasts. Today, for example, he had dined on the finest entrecôte steak he had ever tasted; lunched on a superb braised oxtail printanière; breakfasted on broiled kippers and Wiltshire ba-con. Was there anything redeeming in his having skipped the midmorning bouillon and afternoon tea? None, he thought. By this time in the evening he wanted little else than to sink into a comfortable chair in the ship's Reading Room. His nightly routine had been established early in the voyage: a long, late dinner, a stroll on the deck, and reading until the early morning hours.

Spearman had selected his reading material with care. He had decided on some of the published works of his acquaintances who were traveling on board. It would be economical to have the authors close enough at hand so that Spearman could question them directly about some point that had engaged his interest or with which he disagreed.

But first the obligatory walk on deck. With one hand sliding along the chrome bannister, Henry Spearman ascended the large staircase outside the entrance to the Columbia Room. It was covered in a carpet of royal blue with a piling deep enough to smother the soles of his shoes. He tugged at the heavy door opening onto the promenade deck and stepped into a dark mist. At first little could be seen. Then Spearman made out a few passengers leaning against the rail. As he walked along, he passed another traveler rug-wrapped in a deck chair, seemingly asleep. Spearman paced briskly. Somewhat to his surprise, the rhythm of shipboard life was much to his liking. The escape it provided from telephones, messages, and mail was relaxing. After the horrible events of the last semester the total change in environment was just what the doctor ordered. Indeed as far as he was concerned, the voyage had gone too fast. But he knew that some thought otherwise. The Webers had complained they felt a bit claustrophobic; Oliver Wu agreed, saying the ocean had become monotonous. With this judgment Denton and Jessica Clegg concurred. Sophie Ustinov and Christolph Burckhardt claimed they had found a few too many shipboard bores; Valerie Danzig apparently had discovered some rather more riveting characters and, like the Spearmans, found little disagreeable about the voyage. As he started on the second lap, Spearman noticed that a slight drizzle had begun. The wind was blowing harder and he could feel the spray from the ocean. Abruptly the temperature seemed to drop and he hunched down against the chilly night air. The ship's motion became more pronounced, and the light streaming from the portholes revealed a gray-black sea with multitudes of whitecaps. The deck had begun rolling and pitching, and it was difficult to make progress against the strong headwind that swept the by-now-deserted promenade deck. Spearman decided that he would return to the ship's interior at the first available entrance door.

He pulled at the handle, but the blowing wind made it difficult to open. Finally it gave way and Spearman entered the corridor accompanied by spray and wind. He heard the door quickly snap back in place, and he faced the warm security of the ship's interior. A carpeted passageway brought him, after some circuitous meandering, to a stairway which he descended to Four Deck. He entered his stateroom and noticed a note lying on the bedspread. It was from Pidge, informing him that she and Jessica Clegg, along with Christolph Burckhardt, had decided to take in the movie in the ship's theatre.

The economist walked into the bathroom and filled the basin. The water slowly rose and fell from side to side in the white enamel sink. For the first time in the voyage the ship's movement had become pronounced as the liner headed into a force-nine gale. Spearman washed his face and hands of the salt residue, left by the spray, that had crusted on his skin, re-entered his cabin and fetched the material from which he would select the evening's reading. He glanced at each title before stuffing it into his briefcase. *The Muse and the Fire of Genius* by Valerie Danzig; Sophie Ustinov's autobiography, *Compounds and Mixtures: My Life as a Chemist; Mores and Manners Among the Melanesians* by Denton Clegg; Calvin Weber's *The Conrad Nobody Knows; Bets and Numbers: Mafia Control of Urban Gambling* by Oliver Wu; and, finally, *Adventures in Philately* by Christolph Burckhardt. Then Spearman retrieved a raincoat, cap, and scarf from the closet just in case he might want some fresh air on deck before retiring for the night.

The ship pitched and rolled as Spearman made his way down the corridor of Four Deck to the nearest stairway. Periodically he stopped and seized the handrail to steady himself. The loud creaking of woodwork accompanied his progress up the stairs to Quarter Deck. In the distance he heard the sound of a piano and muted cornet coming from the Queen's Room. He negotiated one more flight to Upper Deck. Out of curiosity he detoured past the Players' Club Lounge and stopped in the entranceway. The room was jammed with customers.

He spotted Sophie Ustinov at a slot machine, one outstretched hand full of quarters, while the other quickly pulled the handle. The clanging of coins pouring down the chute indicated that she was being provided some fuel to keep the machine in action. The economist walked through the lounge and paused in the doorway of the casino adjoining it. He scanned the room. Oliver Wu sat impassively at a roulette table. As the croupier swept away the piles of chips from the numbers his bets had covered, Wu replaced the lost wagers with no visible sign of disappointment. The casino was full of stale smoke, and a damp alcoholic fragrance permeated the atmosphere. Spearman decided it was time to leave. He maneuvered past the photo arcade onto the balcony overlooking the Double Room. The nightclub was a roar of talk. Passengers were in a frolicking mood, wearing tinsel crowns and "straw" hats of plastic and throwing streamers. A loud, brassy trumpet led the orchestra in a Gershwin tune, while a leggy female vocalist tried gamely to be heard above the din, intoning the words:

> S-o-o-o-n our little ship will come sailing home,
> Through every storm never failing,
> The day you're mine this world will be in tune,
> Let's make that day come s-o-o-n.

That the *QE2* was sailing through a storm was increasingly obvious even in the ship's interior. But that knowledge did nothing to dampen the spirits of the crowd. The entire room soared up on a wave, tilted, and then fell as the bow of the liner smashed down again into the sea. The ship was pitching heavily as Spearman lumbered up a short flight of stairs to Boat Deck. The music of the band faded away as he emerged into a darkened corridor, at the end of which were two large glass doors that opened into a room on the port side of Boat Deck aft. By dint of holding onto the creaking bulkhead, Spearman clambered along the passage. Then he pushed open the door to his sanctuary.

The room was deserted except for the figure of Denton Clegg seated in a soft leather chair. His hand rose in greeting when he saw his friend enter. Clegg was still in his dinner jacket.

Spearman smiled his own hello, and then lurched slightly as the bow of the ship bumped against the heavy swell. He grabbed the back of a chair to steady himself. "Ah, Henry, I've been waiting for you. I didn't think a bit of rough weather could keep you from your favorite retreat."

"Absolutely not," he replied. The economist nestled into one of the large armchairs lining the walls of the paneled interior. "Neither snow nor rain nor heat nor gloom of night could stay this professor from accomplishing the swift reading of the most recent publications of his friends."

Clegg returned his attention to a news magazine. Spearman sat in his chair awhile before reaching into his briefcase to fetch one of the items within. He took the first book his hand touched and pulled it from the satchel. It was a volume he had been reading earlier and he opened it where he had left off. At first he could not concentrate. The lurching of the ship made that more difficult than had been the case on earlier evenings when, in the same random manner, he had selected his evening's reading.

And there was another matter. Spearman was relaxing and enjoying the sea voyage, but the unpleasant events of the past few months were not that easily driven from his consciousness. He had continued thinking of Melissa Shannon. A seemingly sweet and sensible young lady committing two brutal murders for revenge against acquaintances of his. Nothing in economics says that people are always rational. But these acts were *so* irrational. It was hard to see how Melissa Shannon could believe she could, on balance, increase her utility by murdering two people because they had voted against the promotion of her fiancé. Dennis Gossen had done something that from Spearman's perspective was foolish. Now Melissa had only added to the irrationality of the situation by seeking revenge. She hardly could have expected not to be caught. But then perhaps she had been too distraught to reason clearly after all. Irrational actions were difficult for Spearman to handle within the framework of economics where rationality was a basic assumption. The actions of a Melissa

Shannon were like the actions of a fanatic, a person for whom there are no trade-offs in nature. It is all or nothing. No precise calculating at the margin. No weighing of costs and benefits. No give-and-take. No finesse. Economics deals with well-behaved preference functions, what Wordsworth described as "the lore of the nicely calculated less or more." To be confronted with behavior like that of Melissa Shannon was something of a shock to Henry Spearman. For it seemed inconsistent with the precise calculation of gain and loss. It was acting without reckoning the cost. Melissa Shannon seems not to have heeded the nicely calculated less or more.

The *QE2* pitched down and Spearman felt a slight sickening in the pit of his stomach. Within the room there was a creaking of woodwork against the backdrop of the tumultuous roar outside. The economist clutched his chair and decided that a walk around the room would make him feel better.

Steadying himself by holding onto the chairs and tables spaced out along the walls, Spearman made his way around the enclosed space. He walked to the wall and parted the flimsy curtains on the windows that looked out on the port side of Boat Deck. But he could see nothing out of the rain-spattered windows. To take his mind off of his gloomy thoughts and the nausea, he decided to examine the pictures that lined the interior. They were artists' renditions of some Cunard liners. One of them depicted the *Berengaria*, the first Cunarder to be named after a queen (the wife of Richard the Lion Hearted). Until the *Queen Mary* it was the flagship of the line. Next on the wall came the *Aquitania,* in the 1920s the most fashionable of the Cunarders and the last with four funnels. Then the *Queen Mary*, at whose launch the poet John Masefield wrote an ode. Spearman had been informed by one of the bartenders in Midships Bar who had served on the

Queen Mary that it rolled notoriously. "She could roll the milk out of a cup of tea" is how he put it. A not very welcome image at this moment, thought Spearman. Next, the *Queen Elizabeth*, the largest liner ever built, which had distinguished itself as a troopship during the Second World War. On the aft wall Spearman studied the handsome model of the *Russia*, a Cunard ship of 1867 that operated under sail and steam. A bust of Samuel Cunard was situated near one of the windows opening out on the deck. Spearman studied it with admiration. He knew that Cunard started in the business by carrying transatlantic mail by steam. His first ship, the *Britannia*, which made its first Atlantic crossing in 1840, was a wooden paddle-boat. Samuel Cunard was known to be a cautious man whose safety record was enviable. The Cunard line never lost a passenger in peacetime by shipwreck. As the *QE2* rose, pitched and went over on a long roll to starboard, Spearman hoped the record would be kept for at least one more voyage.

Having exhausted the offerings of the room displays, Spearman settled down again into one of the armchairs. He glanced at the watch on his wrist. It was 11:00 p.m., still early enough for a long evening's study. Henry Spearman sat back in his seat and retrieved his book from the side table. Once again he started to read. Clegg's magazine was on his lap and his chin rested on his chest as he napped. Clegg had relaxed a great deal since the trial of Melissa Shannon ended. So had all the others. Spearman wished that he, too, could allow the terrible events of the spring semester to recede in his mind. But somehow this did not happen. Deep in the recesses of his cerebrum he felt that something was amiss in the whole matter of Melissa Shannon and Dennis Gossen. It wasn't simply the fact that two colleagues had been murdered—that would have been deeply traumatic on its own.

But time, combined with the knowledge that justice had been done, should have helped ease the pain. But that was precisely the point. Spearman was more distraught than were his colleagues because unlike them he sensed that justice had *not* been done. The trial and its verdict had not satisfied him. But if he had been forced to articulate his misgivings, he could not have done so. Try as he might, he could not pinpoint the reason for his restlessness. All that he knew was that he had a vague memory of something that gave him the feeling that things somehow didn't fit too well. Something didn't mesh. He tried to settle down. He decided to go back over the series of terrible events in his mind. His inability to solve the problem using logical processes had left him feeling uncharacteristically inadequate. He sat in silent contemplation. The roaring wind outside seemed far away. Only the heavy creaking of the woodwork as the *QE2* shouldered down into the storm broke the silence within.

Henry Spearman sought surcease from his disquietude by returning to his reading. The book that he had tried reading tonight did not catch his interest so he pushed it back into his briefcase and fumbled for another. He opened it to the place where he had left off and found himself looking at material that promised interest to an economist. It had been some time since he had glanced at these pages.

As he read he felt a twinge of annoyance. Something didn't make sense to his well-ordered mind. He wondered if he should start before the place where he had left off in order to pick up the thread of the discussion. He looked back at a page . . . and then another. . . . Could it be? He looked at the pages again and his mind began racing. . . . He read and reread the material.

Then the light dawned.

It was as if the pieces of a great jigsaw puzzle that at one time had seemed intractable now came together into a sensible pattern. Every piece fit together. All at once he knew with as much certainty as he could ever hope to possess that Melissa Shannon was innocent of the murders of Barrett and Bell. Moreover, he now was convinced with just as much assurance that Dennis Gossen had not committed suicide. He was murdered, just as cold-bloodedly as Barrett and Bell. And he knew who the murderer was.

The identity of the murderer did not come as a kind of visceral realization. He knew it as a matter of impeccable logic, a logic that flowed from one of the most firmly entrenched principles in all of economic analysis: consumers maximize their utility. The reliability of that proposition and its amazing predictive power had been demonstrated over and again in so many ways that it was one of the basic building blocks of correct reasoning in Spearman's discipline. But what he had just read were statements, claiming to be factual, that completely contradicted this powerful economic generalization.

Although the full implications of what he had discovered this evening had become blindingly clear, his course of action did not. What should he do? He needed to think. The Reading Room seemed hot and stuffy and that, along with the pitch of the liner, made him feel dizzy and uncomfortable. A walk on the gusty deck might help clear his brain. Then he would tell Pidge of his conclusions. Together they would think of a plan. He looked round to his companion. The Dean was no longer dozing.

"Is everything all right, Henry?"

"Why do you ask?"

"Because I happened to be looking your way while you

were engrossed in your reading and I noticed that you jumped a little. As if you were startled. Then you seemed completely preoccupied with your thoughts."

"I need some fresh air and some time to collect my thoughts. Then I'll want to discuss with you the problem that's bothering me. Will you be remaining here for awhile?"

Clegg looked at Spearman intently. "If you'd like me to. I want to help you out any way I can, my friend. Knowing you as well as I do, I realize it's something serious."

Spearman started to say something. Instead, after placing the book onto the nearest table, he wrapped a scarf around his neck and muffled into his heavy raincoat. Then he pulled a large cap over his ears. "I'd appreciate it if you'd watch my briefcase." And then he struggled from the room.

When he pushed open the door onto the deck, he felt a tremendous draft blowing. The inrush of wind brought with it a heavy spray which caught Spearman by surprise. He stepped onto the wet, glistening deck and heard the heavy door close quickly behind him. Spearman grabbed the handrail. The long narrow Boat Deck was dimly lit and Spearman could see that it was deserted. The deck went up on a rise of the ship and then fell again, like an elevator. He peered into the ocean. The lights from portholes revealed hordes of angry whitecaps atop the ink-black swell. He breathed deeply. The mistlike spray that was blowing into his face was astonishingly refreshing. He appreciated the wind and the smell of salt air after the mustiness of the Reading Room. He was determined to negotiate his way around the pitching deck while he cleared his brain and made some hard decisions. Slowly and carefully he edged along the rail. Now he could straighten out and maneuver his way along. It took almost thirty minutes to reach the bow, round it, and head down the starboard side toward the stern. He clambered along the blustery promenade deck, his scarf wildly blowing in back of him. Above the crash of the water he could hear little. His mind was so full of thoughts about utility maximization and murder that he didn't notice the passing of time. He was still uncertain as to how to proceed. Various plans revolved in his mind. There was a murderer aboard the liner, and he had no doubt at all as to who it was. Action was imperative. An innocent young woman was suffering in prison. And a killer was loose who might kill again. Deep in thought, he made a complete circuit of the deck and started another. The bow of the ship crashed against the waves and the wind roared.

He did not notice that the door to the Boat Deck had been opened, and he did not hear it close. Nor did he hear the footfalls ahead of him. But then he thought he saw something. The long, narrow deck was dimly lit. On a down tilt he dimly perceived a figure hurrying to the stern. Then a high wave broke over the deck and Spearman was drenched. A chill went through him. The spray in his eyes had momentarily cut off his vision. He wiped his eyes and looked down the deck again. Transfixed, he watched as a familiar figure eased itself over the handrail, hesitated a second, and then, with a shrill scream, leapt into the churning black ocean. Laboriously, Spearman made his way to the part of the rail where the figure had jumped. Shading his eyes, he peered overboard. Only an oily blackness was visible in the tumultuous sea.

Henry Spearman tugged hard at the first entrance door he could find, entered a tangled passageway, and headed for the Reading Room. He pushed open the glass door and looked around. The room was empty. On the writing table near where Denton Clegg had been seated were two envelopes. One was addressed to Jessica Clegg, the other to Henry Spearman. The

economist removed his soaked cap and dripping scarf and
coat. Emotionally depleted, he sat down in a leather chair.
He pulled the unglued flap out of the envelope and shakily
removed the letter inside. It was in Denton Clegg's
handwriting:

Dear Henry:

As you already know, I murdered Dennis Gossen,
Morrison Bell, and Foster Barrett. Even as I write these
words, they seem almost unbelievable to me, as if I am
writing words dictated by someone else. Of all the people
I know, Henry, you could probably best understand (although surely not approve) of my actions. The terror of
being exposed as a fraud outweighed the terror of murdering others to keep from being discovered. Once the
decision was made to protect myself, my career, and all
that had any meaning to me, I went about the business
of murder in the most systematic and disciplined manner.

Killing another was not pleasant. It was simply necessary. As I saw it then, and as I see it now, there was
no other recourse. I had, of course, hoped Dennis Gossen's
dispatch would end the matter. A few months ago he
came to me in great agitation, perplexed by some numbers
in my book on the Melanesians. He had picked it up on
an impulse and discovered that it had relevance for his
own research. But the figures made no sense to him and
contradicted almost all of the work done by economists
in the field, including his own. When he first came to
me to discuss it, he wanted clarification, thinking he had
misunderstood my analysis, or thinking that, at worst, I
had been careless. But when he began to question the
work that was to be the capstone of my career, I lost my
composure—I was only too keenly aware that I had con-
cocted those figures out of thin air.

As you know, Henry, my early work in anthropology
brought me some recognition, but I knew I would not
achieve immortality as an anthropologist without a truly

great work, a fundamental study that would be cited for generations. Being the dean of the faculty required too much time to permit the research necessary for a study of world-class dimensions. And being dean meant power—and power is something I enjoy having. I have been a successful dean. But great fame as an anthropologist eluded me and I continued to covet it. When I took leave of absence three years ago to continue my fieldwork in the Santa Cruz Islands, I hoped I would be able to produce a book that would become a classic. It wasn't too long before I found out that I no longer had the stomach for such painstaking observations. I had been out of the anthropological mainstream for too long; I was too old and had lost the dedication to scholarship such a project required. Then I got the idea of simply fabricating data, backing it up with the proper jargon and the authority of an already established reputation. The imprimatur of Harvard also helped.

For a long time I feared that someone might discover my deception. But that seemed unlikely and such thoughts had largely passed from my mind. You can imagine my shock, then, when your junior colleague began to question my results. I was unprepared for it, and my inability to answer his questions gave me away. He realized that I was lying.

Later he returned and offered me a deal. If I supported him for promotion, he would not reveal my secret. It was blackmail of course. But I was delighted to accept his terms, or make him believe that I had done so. For what I needed was to mollify him and keep him from revealing his suspicions to others. Of course I knew that such a deal only gave me time, not long-term security. A blackmailer rarely stays bought. Dennis Gossen would have owned me. There was no alternative but to kill him.

The plan quickly formed in my mind to make it look like a suicide. The motive would be disappointment over his not being promoted. As you know, as dean of the faculty I can overrule the vote of the P and T committee if I desire. And although that is not usually done, I had decided it would happen in the event that Gossen was promoted. As it turned out, that was unnecessary. I simply exercised my right to break a tie and voted against him. The day after we finished our deliberations, I typed a letter telling him that he was promoted. Time was of the essence. It was important that he not learn from you or anyone else on the committee that he was turned down. So I had a courier deliver his letter late in the evening, lessening the chances that the real outcome would be leaked. Meanwhile I asked to see him personally in order to offer my congratulations and solidify our agreement. To Gossen it was to be something of a celebration. The poison I used was injected by syringe. I poisoned him into unconsciousness with ketamine, a pharmaceutical I learned about in the islands from a doctor who used it as an anesthetic. Gossen collapsed quickly. I carried him to his car, attached a hose to the exhaust pipe and made it appear as a suicide. With ketamine, there's no respiratory depression, so he breathed normally. That way his hemoglobin would show the presence of carbon monoxide in case of an autopsy. I retrieved the letter I had sent him (he had not even opened it) and replaced it with the official one. Then I typed a suicide note on his typewriter.

It might amaze you to learn that all this was done with little regret or pangs of conscience. I was surprised myself by the absence of remorse on my part. There was a job to be done and I did it. The alternative—seeing my scientific credibility destroyed—was unthinkable.

But I was not yet totally secure. At your home I learned that Gossen had attempted to contact Foster Barrett. He had done that before our agreement had been reached. Then I learned at the P and T committee meeting that he had contacted Bell also. I could not be sure that these two had been as scrupulous in not hearing him out as they claimed. Bell admitted to having received a package from him, a package that no doubt contained the information about my deception. So I had to put Bell out of the way quickly, despite his statement that he had no intention of reading whatever it was Gossen had sent to him. Barrett too had to go. Luckily for me they had both voted against Gossen's promotion. It was not hard to make the police think that their deaths were the retribution for Gossen's suicide against those who had voted against him. That's why I leaked information about the voting. Your party provided the opportunity for me to steal Melissa Shannon's gloves in order to implicate her. Murdering the two of them was easy. I knew when Barrett ate at home and not at his club; I also knew the pattern of family life and activities at the Bells—the element of surprise helped. And it was easy to get Gossen's letter from Bell's bedroom.

After Melissa Shannon was convicted, I thought the danger to me was over. This sea voyage allowed me to relax more than I had in many months. I noticed you reading and I saw you suddenly sit bolt upright. When you left the Reading Room, I looked at the book you left behind and realized you were reading the same pages in my book that had aroused Gossen's suspicions. I still do not understand how economics could uncover the fact that I had falsified my data, but I knew you were onto me. To be shown to be a fraud is too much for me to bear, even worse than being shown to be a murderer. I thought briefly of killing you, Henry, to protect my reputation. But sooner or later my duplicity would be discovered again by another Spearman or Dennis Gossen who happens upon my book. So I have come to the end. Once again there is only one clear alternative.

I have written a separate, more personal note to Jessica. I know you and Pidge will be a source of strength to her.

Fondly,
Denton Clegg

17
Thursday, June 13

Henry Spearman knew the ship was moving. Yet he could hear no sound from her engines and he felt no vibration from the propellers. Today the sun was shining brilliantly on a blue sea that looked as flat as a Texas highway. The ship was steaming east at better than twenty-eight knots and would be landing in Southampton tomorrow.

"But I still don't understand how you could know from red feathers and pigs and canoes and yams that Clegg was a faker. I mean, what's the difference if a canoe costs 300 red feathers or a million? I don't understand. I would look at such things and say, 'Fine, if Clegg says it, it must be true. So what? He's the anthropologist.' Anyway, the prices could be anything, couldn't they?" Sophie Ustinov was gesticulating, her eyes wide with stupefaction.

The diminutive economist smiled at her question from a small platform on which he was standing in the Q4 Room. In the evening the area on Quarter Deck aft was used as a small nightclub for first-class passengers. In the daytime it became a place to learn bridge or backgammon. It was ideal for holding a small seminar and that is just what Henry Spearman was doing. He realized that once word got out about Denton Clegg's confessions and suicide, he would be inundated with inquiries for the rest of the voyage. Time would be saved by inviting his friends to attend a private session where he could give a full explanation of the events that had transpired on the previous night. For this purpose he received permission from the ship's captain to use the room. That is why Sophie Ustinov, Valerie Danzig, Oliver Wu, Christolph Burckhardt, and Calvin Weber were seated at chairs drawn up next to the stage.

"But that's the point, Sophie, prices can't just be anything. Relative prices—the price of one thing relative to another—are determined by economic forces. Prices respond to those forces in ways that can be predicted by economic theory."

"But, Henry," Oliver Wu felt like an undergraduate again with his hand waving in the air for recognition from his professor, "why should consumers maximizing their utility imply anything about how one good will be priced relative to another? I thought I understood utility theory when you put it in terms of newspaper vending machines, but somehow I can't see its relevance here."

"I'm also in the dark," Valerie Danzig admitted. "Why would Dennis Gossen suspect Clegg of being a fraud after looking at the data in his book?"

Spearman shrugged his shoulders. "What must have caught Gossen's attention was the fact that Clegg's claims about the prices of goods in the Santa Cruz Islands were inconsistent with what Gossen's knowledge of economics would have led him to expect. I did not see the import of the discrepancy right away, although I should have the very moment Leonard Kost informed me that Gossen was dead."

Now it was Calvin Weber's turn to be puzzled. "Why at *that* moment, Henry?"

"Because precisely at that moment I was perusing Clegg's tables showing the prices of various commodities in the Santa Cruz Islands. But I was too distracted at the time to make anything of them. Nevertheless they invaded my subconscious because almost immediately I felt a vague uneasiness about the Dennis Gossen matter. I never believed Melissa Shannon was guilty, for example. The next time I looked at the same figures, it was like a light went on. That happened last night in the Reading Room. That's when everything fell into place."

Spearman paused, then continued. "Clegg reported that yams were an occasional, inexpensive item in the islanders' diet. Canoes were a big ticket item. It takes a large fraction of a family's income to buy a canoe. I knew that Denton Clegg was a murderer because the prices of yams in the Santa Cruz islands varied relatively less than the prices of canoes. The range of yam prices was from four to five red feather belts, a difference of one belt. The canoe prices varied from 780 to 1,100. That is a difference of 320 red feather belts— a 41 percent differential in canoe prices compared with a 25 percent differential in yam prices. But if consumers maximize their utility, the differentials should have gone the other way. The prices of yams should have varied relatively more than the prices of canoes. *That* is the outcome the theory of utility maximization predicts."

"Well, Henry, since I'm the culprit who kept insisting that utility maximization was a tautology with no predictive power, I should be impressed." Valerie Danzig was sitting back in her chair with her arms folded across her chest. "Nevertheless, I don't see the connection you keep making between the price variations and utility-maximizing behavior. I think that is what is still troubling most of us."

"Then let me make the connection clear." Spearman was in his element when he faced the challenge of drawing an unexpected implication from a commonplace economic proposition. "If a Santa Cruz Islander is a utility maximizer, then he or she will search for a lower price until the expected saving from searching one more time equals the cost of visiting one more seller. At that point the Melanesian, or anyone else, will stop searching for another seller and buy from the person who has already quoted the lowest price. This must be the case. If going to another village in search of another seller, on average, will save more than the cost of that visit, the islander would gain by taking the trip. On the other hand, if the probable gain was less than the cost of making that additional search, the Melanesian would gain by *not* making the visit."

"So far I'm with you," Valerie Danzig said. The others nodded their heads and Spearman continued.

"We can also predict that the Melanesians will search more for lower prices when making a major purchase like a canoe than an occasional inexpensive one, like buying a basket of yams. On a canoe a 1 percent saving would be perhaps ten red feather belts; on yams it would be more like one-tenth of one red feather belt of the same quality. So we can expect the average Santa Cruz Islander to search more for low prices when shopping for a canoe than when shopping for yams. Since it is the case that canoes take more of the typical Melanesian's income than yams, any canoe seller who tries to get a high price from customers relative to that of his competitors will find that many customers will move on to find a better deal elsewhere. That would not be the case with yam sellers. Customers would be more willing to stop searching because the savings from visiting an additional yam merchant would be relatively small."

"Let me give you an example closer to home. At the end of last year I spent the better part of a day shopping for a new car. I would not spend anywhere near that much time shopping for a small kitchen utensil. If I can find a dealer who would offer me even a slightly larger discount on a car than some other dealer I had been to, the extra visit would be worthwhile. But that would not be true with an item like a paring knife. Offer me a 50 percent discount on a paring knife, and I won't drive across town to get it. But even a 1 percent discount on a new car is worth looking into. Now millions of consumers act the very same way. And the result is that their shopping behavior keeps the prices of cars rather closely bunched. But not that of paring knives. Now what's true in the Boston area is true in the markets of the islands. Consequently the principle that consumers maximize their utility leads ineluctably to the prediction that the range of prices of yams in the Santa Cruz Islands should vary more than that of the prices of canoes. But what did Clegg's data show? Just the opposite pattern. Either the theory of utility maximization was wrong or Clegg was fabricating his data. Faced with that choice, no economist would hesitate." Spearman paused to await questions. There were none, so he continued.

"When I arrived at the conclusion that Clegg had been cheating, I remembered Dennis Gossen's desperate attempt to see me and the reason for his visit became clear. I also realized that Clegg had a strong incentive to want Gossen out of the way. Then I remembered that Clegg was aware that Gossen had tried to contact Bell and Barrett. I then deciphered the meaning of the entire pattern of events that has caused so much anguish. But Clegg tells that part of the story in his letter to me—which is a matter for the police."

18
Thursday, August 29

Henry Spearman stood at the window of his office looking out at the gray rain that fell in heavy sheets onto the grass and walks below. He remained motionless for a while. Then he turned toward his desk where a partially completed syllabus awaited his attention.

He had agreed to teach a new course in the fall, one that he had not taught for over twenty years. In that period he had been almost wholly absorbed in teaching graduate students at the frontiers of his discipline, keeping them abreast of his latest research and that of others in the field. Now he thought it would be fun to try his hand at imparting the rudiments of economics to students new to the discipline. He had requested that Leonard Kost assign him a section in the Principles of Economics, one that would be limited to thirty students and for which Spearman would have full responsibility. Spearman's request was gratefully accepted by the Economics department which, like some others at the institution, had been criticized by undergraduate students who wanted more exposure to the stars of the Harvard faculty.

The professor sat down again at his desk and read over what he had written on the legal-sized yellow pad. Original sources in the history of economics were interspersed with readings from a standard introductory textbook. The combination, Spearman thought, would give students an appreciation for the development of the discipline into its present form and protect them from thinking that all ideas were new ideas.

The diminutive economist was so absorbed in planning the syllabus that he did not hear the gentle tap at his door. On the second louder rap he glanced up and, in a slightly raised voice, beckoned the visitor in. One of the department's secretaries entered. "I beg your pardon, Professor Spearman, I didn't want to disturb you, but I thought I should bring this envelope over right away. It just came from the Dean's office and is marked 'Personal and Confidential.' "

"That's fine, Hilda, thanks very much." He reached out to take the envelope. When she departed, he withdrew the contents but had scarcely begun to read the memorandum when the phone rang. It was Pidge.

"Henry, I just wanted to remind you that Patty will be coming in from Philadelphia in about an hour. She said she's bringing some champagne to celebrate her promotion at the zoo."

"I'm afraid that you'll have to celebrate without me. My syllabus is only half done and I must have it to the typist by tomorrow morning in order for it to be ready for the first day of class."

"But Henry, Patty will be disappointed."

"I think she'll understand," Henry Spearman replied. "I may be home pretty late, so tell Patty I'll see her and congratulate her tomorrow." He replaced the receiver and returned to the Dean's notice. It was addressed jointly to Valerie Danzig, Henry Spearman, Sophie Ustinov, and Calvin Weber.

Topic: Promotion and Tenure Committee
    In order to maintain continuity with the policies and procedures for promotion followed last year, I am asking each of you to serve once again on the Promotion

and Tenure Committee. In addition, I will be selecting three newcomers in order to bring the committee back to full strength. Under the circumstances, however, I will understand completely if any of you wish to let this cup pass. Please let me have your answer within the next ten days.

At the bottom it was signed, Oliver Wu, Dean.

Henry Spearman held the notice before him for some time. A feeling of melancholy came over him as painful memories flooded back. Once again he rose from his desk, walked to the window and watched the gray rain cascading down. He thought of the tragedy of Denton Clegg, and of the terrible fates of Dennis Gossen, Foster Barrett, and Morrison Bell. The reality of their deaths reminded him of his own mortality and vulnerability. He realized that the marginal utility of his time was beginning to increase rapidly.

His thoughts turned to Patty and Pidge. Then another memory intruded. Near the end of his life John Maynard Keynes was asked if he had any regrets. "Only one," Lord Keynes replied. "That I have not drunk more champagne."

A half-smile crossed Henry Spearman's lips. He retrieved his raincoat and umbrella from the coatrack and left for home.